From the Outside In

From the Outside In

Seven Strategies for Success When You're Not a Member of the Dominant Group in Your Workplace

Renee Blank
and
Sandra Slipp, Ph.D.
with Vincent Ford

AMACOM
American Management Association
New York • Atlanta • Boston • Chicago • Kansas City • San Francisco • Washington, D. C.
Brussels • Mexico City • Tokyo • Toronto

Special discounts on bulk quantities of AMACOM books are available to corporations, professional associations, and other organizations. For details, contact Special Sales Department, AMACOM, a division of American Management Association, 1601 Broadway, New York, NY 10019.
Tel.: 212-903-8316. Fax: 212-903-8083.
Web site: www.amacombooks.org

Library of Congress Cataloging-in-Publication Data

Blank, Renee.
From the outside in : seven strategies for success when you're not a member of the dominant group in your workplace / Renee Blank and Sandra Slipp.
p. cm.
Includes index.
ISBN 0-8144-7981-2
1. Multiculturalism. 2. Diversity in the workplace. 3. Interpersonal relations. I. Slipp, Sandra. II. Title.

HF5549.5.M5 B547 2000
650.1—dc21 *00-038099*

Printed in the United States of America.

Printing number

10 9 8 7 6 5 4 3 2 1

To
Jae Sarah, Ariane, and Martine
R.B.

To
Sam, Elena, and Mark
S.S.

To
my family
V.F.

CONTENTS

ACKNOWLEDGMENTS

The impetus for this book was the positive response to *Voices of Diversity,* written by two of the current authors, Renee Blank and Sandra Slipp. Lectures, training seminars, and book reviews indicated that there was a broad audience for a follow-up book with an emphasis on what members of the diverse workforce could do for themselves to succeed in the workplace. To all those people, known and unknown to us by name, we give our sincere thanks.

In addition, special mention must be made of Jackie Gates, Jean Lee, Heidi Weissman, Walter Vertreace, and Julio Rodriguez for the invaluable information and numerous resources they provided.

For his generous assistance on the book, both in content and format, we are truly grateful to Robert Blank. Thanks, too, to Judith Seto, Samuel Slipp, and Paul Aron for their important insights and advice.

The staff at AMACOM was, as usual, a pleasure to work with. Our sincere thanks to Ellen Kadin, our acquisitions editor, and our agent, Ed Knappman, for their support and understanding.

Hundreds of interviewees, anonymous in the book, and six named "luminaries" were generous enough to tell us their own stories. We are truly grateful to all of them for their enthusiastic willingness to tell us how they moved from "the outside in." This is their book, and we trust that it faithfully reflects their insights, feelings, and hopes for those who will follow their lead.

INTRODUCTION

Being successful in the workplace is not easy for anyone. It's a tough world out there with lots of competition, local and global. That's why there are so many books and articles about career development and gurus with advice on how to "make it" in the workplace.

But there is always a piece of the career puzzle that's missing from those books and those gurus. The missing piece is how to overcome the extra barrier to success, the barrier—and often it's a big one—caused by being "different" from the dominant group in your workplace. The differences we are referring to here are in race, gender, age, religion, ethnicity, disability, sexual orientation, or language. The purpose of this book is to help people to be successful in the workplace despite this extra barrier of being an outsider.

The barrier for being an outsider has been called the glass ceiling because there is often a limit to how high one can go in an organization. Some call the barrier a concrete ceiling because the level beyond middle manager seems insurmountable. The glass ceiling can at least be cracked—not so the concrete ceiling. Thus, the authors are fully aware of the many real barriers to success faced by people not in the dominant culture.

Nevertheless, some of the glass ceilings are cracking, and even the concrete ceilings are showing some breaks. The time is ripe for taking advantage of the opportunities that are opening up and, indeed, for creating new opportunities. Despite the difficulties, it *is* possible to make it—with a difference. The challenge is to know where and how. That is what this book is about.

First, some background. Several years ago, two of the current authors, Renee Blank and Sandra Slipp, wrote *Voices of Diversity: Real People Talk about Problems and Solutions in a Workplace Where Everyone Is Not Alike.* The purpose of that book was to help managers understand the perspectives, experiences, and treatment of nine different groups of employees in the workplace: Asian-Americans, African-Americans, Latinos, immigrants, workers with disabilities, younger and older workers, gays and lesbians, women, and white men. The focus of *Voices of Diversity* was that the onus was on managers and supervisors to deal with these differences so that both the employees and the organizations in which they worked could benefit.

Only as an aftermath to our original intention did we introduce a chapter titled "When You Are the Other—When You Are Not of the Dominant Culture," to illustrate the responsibilities and opportunities for employees of "difference" for their own success. But much to our surprise, it was this chapter that engaged many of our readers. It was this chapter that *The New York Times* chose to reprint in a special section, "Diversity in the Workplace." And indeed, with our work in organizations we saw a new emphasis on the diversity issue. It was not only what the organization can do for you—as an Asian-American, African-American, Latino, woman, older worker, and so on. It was what you can do to ensure your own success. Forget the "victim" phenomenon and the blame game. It can't help you. Others of your group have made it, and you can too.

Are you asking, "Why should it be the responsibility of employees of difference to adapt, change, or strategize when they are often victims of crude assumptions or, worse, experience outright discrimination?" The reasons are simple and straightforward. As indicated above, there are both opportunities and barriers in the workplace. Interviews for both *Voices of Diversity* and this book, *From the Outside In,* made it apparent that successful members of diverse groups have a clear understanding that one of the first steps for breaking the yoke of "victimhood" is for each person to take responsibility for his or her own career, for being one's own catalyst for change. This proactive approach was always emphasized—and repeated—by those who had moved "from the outside in."

Is there a message here? Are there discrete, learnable strategies and tactics that can be captured and passed on to others trying to make it? The answer is a resounding yes.

So this book is a sequel to *Voices of Diversity,* or more accurately, a counterpart. It captures the ideas, stories, and strategies of "others" in organizations from the perspective of taking charge and taking responsibility for their own success.*

*This book takes some of the same workplace scenarios from *Voices of Diversity*, but reverses the perspective. Instead of relating what management can do to help the person of difference, *From the Outside In* tells what *you* can do when you are not a member of the dominant group in your workplace.

It must be stated emphatically that success or "making it" is defined differently by different people. We want to avoid the notion that success is measured only by the title of CEO or vice president of a Fortune 500 company. This would severely limit the appeal of this book and not speak to the vast majority of workers who have ambitions—simple or grand—that have not been reached. Rather, we sought to learn about success in the stories of those who overcame obstacles to achieve recognition, better assignments, promotions, and increased salaries.

A special caveat: In the book we describe group tendencies. But, as we all know, not all members of a group share the same beliefs, values, and behaviors. Moreover, this book is not intended to be a definitive study of every group discussed. Instead, it makes use of some distinctive tendencies in each group to demonstrate how these tendencies may affect personal interaction, teamwork, and promotional opportunities in the workplace.

For some group members, the issues discussed in the book may not apply. But this book is written for those who have experienced problems and barriers that may be related to their group membership.

This book is based on the accumulated stories of successful people that we have heard in more than twenty years of management consulting, as well as in the many interviews carried out specifically for this book. The following are the criteria we used for categorizing those we interviewed as "successful" who were unusual in the sense that they were successful where many others of their group had not been:

- Member of one of the following groups of workers: African-Americans (also called blacks), Asian-Americans, Latinos, recent immigrants, older workers, gays or lesbians, workers with a disability, or women.
- The first, the only, or one of only a few of their group at a high level in the organization.
- Working in a mainstream organization, not an advocacy agency for their group. (We did not include people successful in an advocacy organization for their own group, such as the NAACP, the Hispanic Federation, or the Asian-American Legal Defense Fund unless they had been previously successful in a mainstream organization or if they were currently instrumental in directly helping members of their group be successful in the workplace.)

We did not include successful people who are in business for themselves, unless they had previously been successful within an organization. Although entrepreneurship is increasingly an important avenue for "outsiders," there are special skills required to be in business for oneself that are different from those needed to be successful within an already-existing organization.

The seven strategies for success developed for this book grew out of the hundreds of stories we heard. We searched for themes and trends and decided that there is, indeed, a consensus on the strategies necessary for "making it," however the success is defined by each individual.

Except in our last chapter, "Have a Vision," the names used are all fictitious to protect the anonymity of those interviewed. The workplace scenarios and success stories in earlier chapters are based on real people with names and, occasionally, professions altered to provide anonymity. Actual names are used in the "Vision" chapter so that those who have been successful can serve as dramatic inspirations for the reader.

Format

This book is a "how-to" book presenting seven strategies that successful people, who were "others" in their organizations, used to move up in the organization. For each strategy, we present an overview of the issue and the rationale for why the particular strategy is important for success. This will be followed by several typical workplace scenarios—two, three, or four—involving obstacles faced by the worker. The scenario will be analyzed, and the reader will be shown how the person could have turned the situation to his or her advantage by using the particular strategy.

Following the scenarios are success stories wherein workers use the strategy to move up within the organization or in a different organization. (Sometimes people have to leave an impossible situation in order to be successful!) These success stories will be described in the "voices" of the group members so that members of each group can see how the story applies to them and how others in their group have succeeded. Occasionally, the voices of mavericks will be expressed so that readers will learn how exceptions to the rule have made it, too.

In addition to workplace scenarios and success stories, we include an elaboration of the strategies with many very specific examples of how the strategy can be implemented. Sometimes we end a chapter with an acronym that captures the essence of the strategy's theme and summarizes the strategy's main points. Our goal is to be highly practical and as "real" and understandable as possible. Let it be noted that we do not want to present a Pollyanna approach that sounds too easy. Rather, we present realistic strategies that may result in a high cost in time, energy, and psychological adjustment but, for all, will yield long-range career benefits and rewards.

Audience for the Book

This book will appeal primarily to employees who perceive themselves as outsiders within an organization because of their group membership and who are looking for ways to become successful despite their "difference." Others who will find the book of interest are managers and mentors who want to maximize the abilities and resources of their employees. This book will be a guide for them in helping employees grow and develop. Effective managers are always good career development coaches for their employees. This book will add to the managers' repertoire of skills to help workers overcome special barriers. The strategies can be discussed in supervisory or feedback sessions, with a suggestion for the employee to read the book or particular section with a follow-up meeting to talk through some ideas of mutual interest.

Summary

While opportunities for advancement are increasing, paradoxically people of "difference" need more and more help in moving "from the outside in." Although there is now increasing awareness in some high places of the value of diversity in the workplace, there is a parallel development of a "leaner, meaner, and less loyal" workplace that makes it harder for all employees to fashion a successful career. The residue of discrimination and stereotypical thinking along with the new workplace mentality requires the mustering of all the knowledge and skills available. It is time for individuals to know, more than ever, that they must take responsibility for themselves to "make it happen." This book, *From the Outside In*, will, we hope, make an important contribution to that end.

From the Outside In

STRATEGY 

CHECK YOUR BAGGAGE

Don't Assume Everyone Is Hostile Because of Previous Bad Experiences —Yours or Someone Else's

Unfortunately, many people of "difference" have had negative experiences—they have been victims of discrimination or stereotypic treatment. And they hear about the negative experiences of others. This "baggage" of experience and memories—your own or others'—influences the way you interpret the present. Bad memories can make you assume that negative experiences will keep happening. You may assume the existence of hostility when it's not really there.

Do people of the dominant culture say things that are hurtful? Of course! Does that mean they are deliberately trying to insult you? Not always! The assumption of guilt may be wrong. Perhaps the person is ignorant or insensitive and doesn't realize how his or her comment or behavior makes you feel.

Yes, of course there is discrimination—racism, sexism, ageism, homophobia. That's a fact of life. *But it's not there all the time.* Not every comment, action, or inaction has a hidden agenda. Not every individual has racist, sexist, or other discriminatory beliefs. Some unfortunately are simply ignorant—they just don't know any better. Others are just callous—but that's life! If you assume that everyone is hostile, if you expect to find discrimination around every corner, you will end up defeating your main goal, which is *your becoming a success.*

Therefore, you must learn to check your baggage—that is, your life's experiences—both yours, and that inherited from others. For many people not of the dominant culture, this may be perplexing advice—easy to understand, yet hard to practice. Even though the number of *overt* discriminatory acts that occur in the workplace may be decreasing, many people continue to carry their own and others' baggage of assumed racism and discrimination.

Other people's baggage can be especially dangerous. Airline personnel question us as to whether or not we have accepted any baggage from strangers. Why? Because that's how bombs have made their way into planes and caused mass destruction. The same is true in our work lives. If we accept someone else's baggage, we run the risk of carrying an explosive device that could detonate at the slightest provocation. And who is hurt? Not the person who provided the baggage; he or she is far away, in a safe place. It's you, the person who accepted the baggage.

So it's important that you "check your baggage"—negative life experiences and stories—and *judge each new experience on its own.* But there's a catch to this advice.

How do you judge the difference between (1) insensitivity due to lack of awareness or knowledge and (2) blatant hostility and discrimination? Why is it important to know the difference? Because how you *define* the situation determines how you *react to* the situation, and your reaction may determine your chance for success in the organization. And that's the bottom line.

If you incorrectly assume that someone is blatantly hostile, you may get angry and react strongly. If this happens, others may think you are "unstable," "too sensitive," or "too emotional," that you have "an attitude" or are "just too difficult to work with."

This friction may create interpersonal problems between you and the other staff, but, just as seriously, it will create problems for *you*. If you get upset over the perceived hostility, you may become stressed out and anxious and less productive in your work.

Even if you don't react openly to perceived hostility but instead swallow it, keep it inside, and do nothing, you are still increasing your level of stress. Doing so may affect your health or may cause you to unnecessarily give up your job.

Let's be clear here. For this strategy, we will *not* be talking about how to react when someone is clearly and blatantly discriminatory, insulting, or offensive. That will be dealt with later in Strategy 5, "Buy In, Don't Sell Out," and in Strategy 6, "Know Your Rights."

Here, we will be talking about the importance of not making assumptions about others' intent that may cause you to overreact to a comment or to someone's behavior. "Checking your baggage" requires an accurate self-assessment. Are you putting a hostile connotation to what is really a stern reaction to some workplace error of yours? If someone seems hostile to you, could there be a legitimate reason?

Self-assessment is not an easy task, but it is a necessary one. You must get a reality check on your skills, abilities, and achievements from trusted colleagues. You must honestly assess the organizational culture and see if there is a fit between the institution's standards of performance and yours.

Self-assessment means empowering yourself to trust others—until you have reason not to. And just how do you do that? First, you must find a way to communicate openly and honestly with people. Being able to do so is one of the most frequently identified traits of successful people. When something bothers you, you must learn to approach the "hostile" person calmly and directly. Instead of harboring resentment, be honest and let the person know how you perceived the words or behavior.

Trust that the other person will receive your feedback with an open mind. This can happen only if you *believe* that you should educate ignorance, not punish stupidity. Yes, sometimes people say or do things out of insensitivity; they just don't realize the effects of their remarks or actions. But how will they learn, unless they are told directly by others, and not through the grapevine?

There are instances when you may be offended or hurt—and legitimately so. You may have been ignored or not invited to a function, or you may have overheard a stereotypic remark about someone of your ethnic or racial group. But the "punishment" (your reaction) should fit the "crime" (what the other person said or did). Let's not react with an atom bomb when a pea-shooter may be enough!

Let's now look at some real-life workplace scenarios and how people *responded and should have responded* to perceived hostility and negativity.

Scenes from the Workplace

WHAT'S IN A WORD? "IT'S JUST BUSINESS, NOT PERSONAL"

Mike Hernandez is a hard-driving Latino director of sales at an appliance manufacturing company. His technical expertise is unquestioned within the organization. Jaime Rodriguez, a close work associate and twelve-year veteran of the organization, tells Mike about all the "problems" he has had with management in general and Bruce Ward, the vice president, in particular. Mike has heard these comments and war stories of discrimination and racism so often that he now "carries" these situations as his own.

At a recent meeting, Mike finds himself recalling several of Jaime's war stories after what he perceives as an insensitive, racist remark by Bruce. Mike explodes at Bruce, totally catching his boss off guard. This is the encounter:

During a product planning meeting, discussions of "special markets" are lively. On several occasions, Bruce says, "Let's be sure to create an eye-catching package. You know that Latinos like to wear loud colors—even if they don't blend or match." He chuckles lightly but obviously. He continues his instructions to the group by saying, "We should be sure to hire a woman model who possesses all the typical Puerto Rican features. We want to make certain that no one mistakes our model for a Caucasian woman—that would ruin the image."

Mike is enraged. He immediately takes offense at his boss's words and says, "How dare you make such racist comments about my people? I don't appreciate your words or tone of voice—or did you think I wouldn't understand English?" The rest of the people in the room are stunned—not by Bruce's comments but rather by Mike's reaction to them.

Everyone just sits waiting for the volcanic eruption from Bruce, and their expectations are met. The battle lines are drawn. The V.P. immediately responds, "Mike, in my office—now! Your public display is inappropriate and inexcusable. Let's go." With this, Mike grabs his folder and admonishes the person taking the minutes of the meeting, saying, "Make sure you get all of his comments on the record. I don't want him denying his remarks." The meeting recorder is stunned and petrified. He doesn't want to take sides and certainly doesn't want to cross Bruce, who is his boss too.

What just happened? Were Bruce's comments racist? Or was he trying to be sensitive to a market and provide packaging that he felt would boost sales? Should unintended slights be ignored? Are they any less painful? Will direct confrontation over this issue be beneficial? What do you think? What would you have done?

What Should Mike Have Done?

Mike might have done the following:

1. Mike had never had a problem with his boss before. Unfortunately, war stories and organizational folklore, which oftentimes are greatly exaggerated, can shape the behavior of otherwise well-meaning people who have not personally experienced racism or discrimination and cause them to overreact to situations. This assumption of hostility in an organization is not only unfair to the alleged "offender" but also crippling to the person who overreacts to the alleged offense. Mike should have remembered his favorable experiences with Bruce.
2. Mike should have realized that he was probably carrying Jaime's "baggage," as well as his own. Without this "baggage," Mike might have tempered his remarks to his boss and thus been more effective. Instead, his inner voice heard the explosives that Jaime had continually given him before anything even had happened to Mike himself.

3. Mike's choice of behavior could have ranged from passive (ignoring the comment) to aggressive (responding in an angry manner, as he did). Fortunately, there are several behavioral options between the passive and aggressive choices:
   a. For example, Mike could have chosen to educate his boss, in private, about the fact that his comments could be perceived as insensitive at best or racist at worst. Mike could have explained why he and others might feel that way. This approach delivers the message to his boss without personally accusing him of insensitivity or racism. In this way, Mike would have assumed that Bruce acted out of ignorance, not malice.
   b. Another assumption Mike could have made was that the comments were personally offensive—perhaps not to others, but to him. In that case he could have assertively told his boss—in private, while avoiding the term "racist"—that he was uncomfortable with those comments and that he would appreciate it if they were not made in the future. This technique would have allowed Mike the ownership of his feelings and directed the conversation and anger at his boss as an individual.
   c. Mike should have realized that, in addition to the words he used with his co-workers and his boss, his nonverbal communication was equally important and needed to be controlled. Communications experts say that 85 percent of communication is nonverbal: facial expression, voice tone, eye contact, body movement, and posture. In the scenario presented, Mike spoke sarcastically and very critically. He probably raised his voice. We can only imagine his facial expression; he probably showed anger and contempt. He might have stomped out of the room, showing tension in his body movements. This might have been construed as aggressiveness, even potential violence. Mike should have realized that his nonverbal communication might have conveyed to some people that he was out of control. This could frighten some people. Others might conclude that he was simply acting in an unprofessional manner.
   d. Certain organizational realities might have restricted Mike's response. If his relationship with Bruce, his immediate boss, was not good, he might have thought twice about reacting to the comment at all. He might have had to consider whether

the potential consequences of a response would be worse than the offensive words. This is a conscious choice that only Mike could have made.

What Might Mike Have Said to His Boss (in Private)?

Mike might have said the following to his boss in private: "Bruce, the Latino markets, while large and financially stable, are also very sensitive to potentially insulting or condescending remarks and actions. I'm sure it was not your intent to be insulting or condescending, but, as a member of the Latino culture, I, for one, found your remarks about loud, unmatching colors offensive and I am concerned how they could be perceived by others. Everyone has to be aware of stereotypical statements because they might result in the loss of valuable markets as well as poor morale among Latino employees in our company."

RELIGIOUS AND INTERPERSONAL DIFFERENCES: SOURCES OF CONFLICT

Waheed Khan, a recent Pakistani immigrant, is working as a project manager for a software company. A conscientious and capable worker, Waheed brings to his job a full range of technical and managerial experience he gained in Pakistan. And he's very aware of how fortunate he is to be working in the United States as a manager.

But the negatives of this job are getting to him. For one thing, a few co-workers, having little knowledge of the difference between Pakistan and India, refer to him as "the Indian." Moreover, no one seems to understand that devout Muslims (like Waheed) pray several times a day. On one holiday, when he takes time off to attend services at a nearby mosque, one of the other managers says, "I sure hope you aren't praying for that madman Saddam Hussein!" Waheed is embarrassed and insulted by this assumption that, as a Muslim, he's sympathetic to terrorist activities. He scowls and walks away.

The Christmas party is coming up and, as a devout Muslim, he dreads going. He knows that he'll be ridiculed because he doesn't dance with women or drink liquor.

At a meeting with his supervisor, Joe Baker, Waheed blurts out, in a loud and forceful voice, that he's angry about his co-workers' attitude toward him. Joe is not sympathetic and tells him to tone his voice down and work out his problems with his colleagues. Waheed is very disappointed with Joe's response and doubts if he can be successful in this company.

"There's too much prejudice and hostility against Muslims here," he concludes. "I was crazy to expect fairness and understanding about my devotion to Islam."

Are Waheed's co-workers prejudiced and hostile? Is Joe being unfair to Waheed by asking him to "work it out" with the other staff? Waheed doesn't even try to check out his assumptions. He assumes that all the other employees are hostile toward his religion because one or two of them tease him about praying. He doesn't bother explaining himself because he might feel uncomfortable. Moreover, he, like many immigrants, doesn't want others to think of him as strange and different.

What Should Waheed Have Done?

Waheed should have done the following:

1. Waheed should have "checked his baggage"—that is, the assumption that everyone was hostile to him. He should have tried to differentiate among prejudice, discomfort, and insensitivity caused by lack of knowledge.
2. He needed to reflect on the issue of hostile remarks in the workplace, whether said in jest or not, and the appropriate response to them. Frequently co-workers confuse the lines between good-natured banter (a male bonding ritual in many cases) and stereotypical statements that can be emotionally damaging. In either case, the people making offensive remarks should be told that their behavior is hurtful. Non-action by Waheed could have been perceived by others as acceptance of the remarks.
3. Waheed should have analyzed his problem as follows: (a) he valued his job and his relationships with his co-workers and boss, (b) he wanted to defend himself, his family, and religious and ethnic heritage in a way that was respectful to himself as well as to the others,

and (c) he could no longer tolerate the remarks or "jokes" about terrorists and Muslims.

4. If Waheed concluded that the remarks were good-humored in intent, he should have assertively educated his co-workers about the effect their remarks had on him.
5. If Waheed felt that people made the remarks and "jokes" out of malice, knowing that he would find them offensive, he would have had to give more assertive feedback, saying firmly and directly that the remarks were unacceptable. He should also have told his co-workers that, if they didn't stop on their own, he would have to report their actions to his supervisor. (This will be discussed further in Strategy 6, "Know Your Rights.")
6. Waheed needed specifically to ask his supervisor to tell all workers that it is important to understand and accept differences. Ridiculing someone because of his or her background is not acceptable behavior.
7. Waheed should have informed the manager and his co-workers about aspects of his religious beliefs and practices that native-born Americans might be unaware of, such as abstinence from drinking and dancing and the requirements for praying at certain hours. Waheed might want to see himself as a "cultural ambassador," helpful to mainstream American employees who may come into contact with immigrants like himself.
8. Waheed should have informed others that not all Muslims (such as those from Pakistan, Iran, India, and Indonesia) are Arabs and that even Muslims who *are* Arabs by and large do not support terrorism.

What Might Waheed Have Said to His Co-Workers?

Waheed might have said the following to his co-workers: "I don't mind joking around once in a while. But this constant harping on terrorists and Muslims is hurtful. When you continually make these references I feel angry and embarrassed. This doesn't help my work performance any, and ultimately the team suffers. I would appreciate it if you did not make these kinds of statements anymore, even in jest. They are insulting to me and to the other good, hardworking Pakistani—both here and in Pakistan—who are not sympathetic to terrorists."

What Might Waheed Have Said to His Supervisor?

Waheed might have said the following to his supervisor: "I realize there are some misunderstandings between some of the employees and me. Most of the staff doesn't know much about Pakistan or about the Muslim religion. I don't want to stand out and seem to be different, but since I do have a special background, it would be helpful to explain some of this to you and the other workers. I would also appreciate it if you would speak to everyone about the importance of trying to understand different backgrounds and religions.

"I'd also like your help—and feedback—on typical customs and styles in the American workplace. In our culture, speaking in a loud tone is a typical way of talking. Here, people may think I'm angry or rude, but I'm just being forthright. I now see that some people are offended by this, and I will try to tone it down. But I want to know if there is anything else about my behavior that others seem to misinterpret. I can't change my culture and background, but I do want to adapt the way I behave to fit into the workplace as much as possible. I'd like your help in doing that."

• —— •

"MEN, THEY'RE ALL ALIKE"

Lois Kearns and Joan Meyers, both single parents, hold senior management positions in a large hotel. Lois is head of the banquets department and Joan is manager of the accounts division. Their boss, Steven Monroe, the hotel's assistant general manager, has usually been sympathetic toward them and the child care issues they face. He knows that night meetings are a problem for both of them and, if he has to hold one, he tries to give them plenty of notice so they can make arrangements for child care.

The hotel has recently been acquired by a national chain, and a new general manager, Howard Thorndike, has been hired. Steven is relieved that he has kept his job but is concerned because his former boss had given him plenty of authority and autonomy. After meeting with Howard, it is clear to Steven that the management style of the hotel is going to be vastly different.

Howard Thorndike is a take-charge person and immediately lets the staff know that he is going to take a hands-on approach and be responsible for all decisions. He also lets Steven know that he wants to run a tighter ship, with more productivity from everyone.

The first week on the job, Howard calls an "emergency" meeting to be held after 6:00 that same night. Both women complain to Steven. "This is a horror for us," Lois says. Joan joins in, "You know the story—your wife works. We can't just change all our child care arrangements with a couple of hours' notice. Please let Howard know that we need plenty of lead time to change any of our hours. And that it's always been that way."

Steven is worried as he prepares to meet Howard. And his boss fulfills his expectations. "We're running a business here," Howard says, "not a nursery. Either the women are professionals or they're not. If they can't manage the job, there are lots of others to fill it."

When Steven tells Lois and Joan that he is unable to change Howard's mind and that he's very strict on procedures, the women become angry. "Steven," Lois says, "you're our boss and you have lots of input." Joan adds, "I can't believe you would cave in. We thought you understood the new work realities. But I guess you're no different from other men. You all stick together when your own necks are at stake."

What Should Lois and Joan Have Done?

Lois and Joan should have done the following:

1. Lois and Joan should have controlled their anger when Steven told them that he couldn't change the general manager's mind. Their outburst could be seen as unprofessional and could have antagonized Steven, who had worked well with them in the past.
2. The women should have checked their assumptions that Steven was "no different from other men" and that he was not concerned about them. They should not have immediately accused him of misunderstanding the "new work realities."
3. They should not have lumped him together with Howard by saying, "You all stick together when your own necks are at stake." By saying this, Lois and Joan were polarizing the relationships between the men and the women—"us" against "them."
4. They should have had some empathy for Steven and his insecurity with the new manager. Lois and Joan should have expressed sym-

pathy to Steven for his difficulty of being in the middle—between Howard's demands and their need for predictable hours. They should have realized that Steven had less power in the organization than they had attributed to him.

5. Lois and Joan should have asked Steven to work collaboratively with them to come up with some alternative solutions for dealing with last-minute emergency meetings (teleconferencing, e-mail from home). Flex time would have allowed Lois and Joan to stagger hours and have others cover for them.
6. Lois and Joan should have scheduled a meeting with Howard, with or without Steven, to assertively "educate" Howard about the new realities of the workplace, including the need for recognition of the child care responsibilities of the staff. The women should have realized that this was a period of transition for some employees, like Howard, whose work experience may have come from a period of time and a place where women did not play such a significant role in the workplace.
7. Lois and Jean should have assured Howard, the general manager, of their willingness to put in extra hours—but that in most instances they needed advance time to make child care arrangements. They should have taken direct responsibility for their relationship with Howard, emphasizing their commitment to ensuring the success of the hotel.

What Might Lois and Joan Have Said to Steven, the Assistant General Manager?

Lois and Joan might have said the following: "Steven, we appreciate all the support you've given us in the past with our family arrangements, and we know you're on the spot now with new management. Could you set up a meeting with Howard to see how we can accommodate his need for last-minute meetings and our need to meet both our work and home responsibilities? When requesting the meeting, perhaps you can review again our many years of performance excellence on the job and our desire to continue working to our utmost capacity for the hotel's continued growth and success. We're sure we can come up with an equitable means of handling staff communication and some adjustment in meeting hours and attendance."

ISOLATION AND LACK OF SUPPORT: IS THIS HOSTILITY?

Fred La Monte, a black senior engineer, is a recently hired project director who supervises twenty engineers at an information technology company. He had formerly held a similar job in a much smaller company. Although there are several other blacks in this organization, he is the highest-ranking black manager.

Fred feels very confident about his expertise in the field and he welcomes the opportunity to build on his experience and to advance his career.

Four months into the job, Fred feels uneasy. When he first arrived, everyone seemed very cordial, but now he is convinced that he is being excluded from information channels and informal meetings. He sees other people going out together for lunch and chatting during the day. But no one has reached out to him, either to join them for lunch or meet after work for a drink.

He is determined to focus on the job itself. The procedures are somewhat different from those at his last job; he has many questions, but he isn't sure whom to ask. His boss, Tim Patell, the director of technical services, is out of the office much of the time and, when he is there, is preoccupied with some major restructuring in the company and doesn't seem particularly friendly to Fred.

Fred has held several staff meetings but, in these meetings, feels a lack of respect from his subordinates. When he asks for clarification of a procedure, he feels disdain from the group for his lack of information. Twice he has asked his subordinates for reports, and both times they were turned in late. He doesn't know whether the staff generally doesn't work as hard as they should or whether their behavior is a slight to his authority.

Fred feels he is in an environment that is hostile to his success. He's angry and frustrated because he feels he will be seen as nonmanagerial—as someone who can't solve his own problems. He is certain that this hostility to him is based predominantly on race.

What Should Fred Have Done?

Fred should have done the following:

1. Fred should have recognized that he needed a plan for acceptance and for gaining managerial credibility with his staff. He should not

have concluded that all the staff was hostile or racist until he had followed through on his plan.

2. Fred should have asked his boss to set the tone for Fred's acceptance as the new project director. He should have asked his boss to inform his colleagues and subordinates about his background and qualifications.
3. He should have sought out numerous resources to ensure that he had essential information—procedural and substantive—to do the job.
4. He should have introduced himself to other senior management and stated his request to be included in informal meetings, lunches, and extracurricular social activities that were the norm for the company. Fred should have taken the initiative in moving from "outsider" to "insider."
5. Fred should have sought out colleagues, both white and black, for help on how to be successful within the organization. It was important for him to learn how to develop a large network of support of his own, in addition to the support from his immediate boss.
6. Most important, Fred had to "check his baggage"—the assumption that others didn't want him to succeed. He should have realized that it's only in the ideal work world that bosses and subordinates are helpful and go out of their way to ease a new person's path. In most cases, people are too busy with their own concerns and career goals and haven't the time or energy to extend the helping hand. Fred had to make the move himself and not blame all his "problems" on perceived prejudice and racism.

What Might Fred Have Said to His Boss?

Fred might have said the following: "Tim, although you've given me lots of background material on the projects I'll be heading, there are some specifics that I'd like more information on. Can we meet sometime next week for lunch? I would enjoy the opportunity to know more about the staff I'll be working with, the resources available, and any specific advice you have on learning the ropes."

What Might Fred Have Said to Other Department Heads?

Fred might have said the following: "I'd like your help in setting a lunch meeting this week with some of the other senior staff so that I can get to know them better and they can get to know my department and its needs and how we can help each other."

Success Stories

People who are successful often test their assumptions about hostility in the workplace. They ask themselves: are people really hostile or are they just busy, or uncomfortable with someone who is "different"? Are seemingly hostile people just teasing the "other" or simply unaware of being insensitive?

Listen now to Jack, Lori, Pam, and Tricia, "success" stories who used Strategy 1, "Check Your Baggage," to their advantage.

THE DISCOMFORT FACTOR

Jack Walters, an African-American attorney and the highest person of color on the legal staff of a large utility company, felt isolated and alone. He was surely the "other." All the black senior staff sat together at lunch and public functions. He had heard from other blacks in the company that the industry culture was "anti-minority." When he visited a competing company, he noticed the same phenomenon; there was little interaction between whites and blacks on the management level.

Jack saw this as a challenge. "Maybe it wasn't hostility from others; maybe it was just discomfort," he said. "I decided to try different things to reach out to white colleagues. I am a golfer, and I put some golf literature and a trophy on my desk. I knew a few of my peers had to pass my desk occasionally and I thought this might be a conversation starter. I was right. Jim and Tom, two of the white attorneys, glanced my way the first day I put these golf mementos out and seemed delighted to stay and chat about our mutual interest. They casually mentioned lunch—just threw it out—and I jumped at it. I learned something. You can't assume everyone is out to get you or resents you. I don't know if I'll ever be close buddies with them, but we do have a relationship.

They've helped me with lots of subtle stuff I just didn't know about because I was out of the mainstream. We talk plenty of golf—that's the opener—but it has led to invaluable advice and support. You've got to check out your assumptions—take the lead. *Not everyone is hostile!*"

We realize that cynics are reading this and asking why the minority person had to make the move first. Why didn't the people from the dominant culture make the first move or take the first step?

Why does the minority always have to don the robe of the majority culture? Why can't the dominant culture ever take on the robe of the minority culture? These are good questions to ask and ponder. All we ask is that you get in touch with your ambitions and then ask yourself what strategy is going to advance them—taking overt action yourself or waiting for the people of the dominant culture to meet you in your world. Is it fair for you to make the first move? Fairness is not the issue—success is!

"NO CINDERELLA HERE; I'M NOT WAITING TO BE RESCUED"

Lori Stern, an experienced quality control manager in an aerospace corporation, the only female among her peers, was ready to "kill." When she met with other staff at meetings and conferences, the informal conversations were always about sports, or she invariably had to suffer through conversations with veiled innuendoes about her male co-workers' sexual encounters with their girlfriends.

She often wondered, "Are they talking like this because they consider me one of the boys, or is it to demean me and make me feel like less of a professional?" "Either way," she said, "I felt a constant hostility and antagonism toward me. But the worst thing I had to face was that I was invariably ignored when I made suggestions at peer meetings. In the few cases where I wasn't ignored, others took up my ideas and took credit for them.

"I had three tasks ahead of me. I had to deal with this sexual innuendo, with sports conversation stuff, and I had to appear credible. As for the sports conversation, I decided to join them, not fight them. I appeared interested and even picked up some knowledge along the way. Listening to sports is not the worst thing, and I can't assume it's sexist and an attempt to isolate me. On the sexual stuff, I nonconfrontationally asked them to quit it and keep that talk for after work. It was the lightness of my style that seemed to work. So the social chitchat took a turn for the better.

"On the credibility issue, I needed a strategy. I decided not to see this as hostility—to check that baggage. I asked Ben, the man who hired me, for feedback. 'I don't want to be a spoilsport or petty,' I told him, 'but I'm not getting my ideas across, and others seem to pick them up and run with them.' He gave me feedback on how to be more forceful and supported me at meetings. The next time someone took my idea I smilingly called it to everyone's attention and said, 'It's great you're picking up on my idea, which I mentioned an hour ago'—*and the strategy worked*. Best, I felt good about myself because I took the initiative to change the situation. I found someone who was sympathetic and wanted to help. No Cinderella complex here. I'm not waiting to be rescued. You've got to be active on your own behalf!"

EDUCATE OTHERS—THEY DON'T UNDERSTAND

Pam Cortez, a director of marketing and the first Latina senior executive in her furniture chain, empowered herself by trusting others. "When someone says or does something that I find insulting or hurtful, I approach that person directly," she said. "I take people where they are, attributing what might be regarded by others as digs or stereotypical remarks as ignorance or insensitivity. Once when my boss complimented me on a project and said, 'That was great. I never knew a Hispanic person could do that,' I answered, 'How many Hispanics or Latinos do you know?' My boss was startled and said, 'You're right. I don't know many at all. It was ridiculous of me to say that.'

"Up to that time, my relationship with my boss had been good, but strictly professional. This incident broke the ice, and our trust and respect for each other as people greatly improved."

RUSHING TO JUDGMENT IS A MISTAKE

Tricia Silva is a newly hired executive secretary for a small cosmetics firm. "I thought my new boss, Greg Inman, would be great," she said. "He was a smiling kind of guy, very friendly and considerate. It was obvious to me from the time he hired me that he liked me. But I was worried that it was not only for my organizational and computer skills.

"I'm twenty-seven, and I know many men think I'm attractive. My family and friends think I'm uptight in many ways, and maybe I am. But I had real problems on the last job with two of my co-workers who pestered me about going out with them. They 'kidded around' by getting close to me in the corridors and always eyeing me up and down. I made an excuse about having a boyfriend, but it didn't seem to do any good; they were always coming on to me. When I had this chance for a promotion in another firm, I grabbed it. 'It's a great opportunity,' I thought, 'and I'll get away from those pests.'

"But now, on this new job, I thought I might have gotten into the same situation as before. I was concerned about my boss. Greg was not obnoxious, but he complimented me very often. Yes, it was on my computer skills, but also on my dress and even once on my perfume. But I wasn't interested in him. He was older and not attractive in my eyes. And I also knew that it was not a good idea to go out with a supervisor; if he did ask me out, I wouldn't go.

'I really like this job. Am I being too sensitive?' I thought. 'Am I overreacting to a guy just because he's friendly and complimentary? If men are genuinely friendly and supportive, does this mean that they're coming on to me? Am I too uptight?'

"I decided to check my assumptions with other women in the department. I asked them, 'Do you consider him a flirt? Does he come on to you?' All the women denied that he was in any way offensive to them or other women in the company. They said that they had observed his behavior with me and it was no different from the way he treated the other women.

" 'Greg is just a very warm, friendly, considerate boss,' they said. 'He's a happily married man and very supportive of women. His wife works and he understands the child care issues that women face.'

" 'But I'm uncomfortable with his compliments about my appearance,' I said. 'So tell him that,' I was advised.

"And I did that. The next time he told me how great I looked, I said, 'Greg, I know you're just being friendly and probably don't mean anything, but your remarks about my appearance make me feel uncomfortable. I hope you don't think I'm uptight, but that's just the way I am.'

"Greg looked startled but told me that he really appreciated my telling him how I felt and that, of course, he wouldn't do that again. I was concerned that our professional relationship might change, but I had nothing to fear on that account. He still is as supportive of me as ever and recently sent me to an advanced computer training program.

"I have learned that you can't generalize about men. One offensive experience with men at the workplace doesn't mean that all men are coming on to you sexually. A compliment can simply be a well-meaning compliment. I also learned that if you say 'please stop' in a nonjudgmental way, it can sometimes be a win-win situation, as it was with Greg. By working it out with Greg, I avoided a situation that could have been detrimental to my career."

Principles of "Checking Your Baggage"

We've looked at some workplace scenarios and success stories in using Strategy 1, "Check Your Baggage," and handling others' insensitivities. Are there some general principles we can derive from these workplace examples? Yes! These principles can be found in two categories: internal and external.

The Internal Principles

Checking your baggage and the appropriate response to other people depends on your reactions to the "offense," your analysis of the situation and the person who caused the offense, and the risk factors in responding. Let's look at some ways of strategizing that each person must decide on. They are:

- Don't erase it.
- Don't nurse it.
- Don't curse it
- Don't rehearse it.
- Try to disperse it.

Don't Erase It

Let's start there. It's important psychologically to *own* and recognize your hurt and then decide how to handle it. Otherwise, it will fester in the back of your mind and come out angrily when you least expect it. After you're aware of your feelings, decide whether you're just carrying old "baggage" or not. Make a conscious decision as to how to act. Don't be in denial. Be in charge. Weigh the *consequences* of your response. Jack, Lori, Mike, Waheed, Fred, Joan, Lois, Pam, and Tricia all felt hurt by colleagues' reactions to them. But only Jack, Lori, Tricia, and Pam—the "success" stories—decided to *test* their perceptions of hostility.

Mike, Waheed, Joan, Lois, and Fred may have recognized their feelings, but they didn't weigh the consequences of their reactions—or lack of reactions. Remember, Mike and Waheed expressed their anger directly without weighing the intent of their bosses' remarks or the consequences of their own responses.

Don't Nurse It

That is, don't go off into a corner and lick your wounds and exaggerate the significance of the slight. Yes, you need to heal, but don't embellish the scenario or add your unique interpretation to explain why someone said or did whatever. Keep an open mind when you attempt to diagnose the reasons why another person hurt you. Moreover, you may end up labeling the individual and furthering a stereotype—which is unfair and exactly what you don't want done to you. Rather, take the higher ground; if at all possible, recognize the infraction and educate the person if you feel comfortable doing so.

Remember, if someone says something derogatory, it may be part of the organizational culture to "put people down." Everyone is fair game for name calling—to be "one-up." Race, age, sexual orientation, gender—all may be used to "get at you" and give the other person an advantage over you. Check out the organizational culture, so you at least will know if you are dealing with an organizational or individual issue. If it is the former, you may have to decide whether or not you can tolerate such an organization.

Some people honestly don't realize they are being offensive. They assume that their beliefs are facts; they don't realize that they hold stereotypes or misinformation about groups. For example, as shown in the scenario about Waheed, some people don't know the difference between India and Pakistan. Many are unaware of the requirements for a devout Muslim. In Mike's case, his boss had stereotypical views about how Latinos dress. Many people are open to—and even welcome—new information, as long as it's not provided in an accusatory manner. As to Howard, the new general manager, he may have been unaware of or insensitive to the changing realities of women in the world of work.

Remember, too, as in the case of Fred, the African-American engineer, that what seems like a putdown or a rejection may simply be a result of another person's just being busy or preoccupied, or it may be part of the normal process of getting credibility when new on a job. Fred, as well as Mike and Waheed, had some baggage from the past that may have influenced his perceptions of co-workers.

Don't Curse It

Don't fall victim to the "all those people are like this" syndrome. Or the "I knew this would happen" syndrome. Fred, Mike, Waheed, and Lois and Joan probably fell into this pattern. This blaming and distancing behavior only makes matters worse and precludes any amicable solution. If you charge discrimination, you'll have to prove it—and the subtle, insidious kind may be hard to prove.

Fight discrimination when it is clear cut and explicit (as described in Strategy 6, "Know Your Rights"). Don't let your anger be so corrosive that it slowly eats away at you. If you do, it could later become explosive and destructive behavior—to yourself and others.

It is imperative, also, that you do not let your own experiences or someone else's baggage influence you as it did with Mike, who was undoubtedly influenced by Jaime's warnings about Bruce Ward, the V.P. Make a judgment about your treatment based on your *own* perceptions and about a particular, specific incident. Someone else's experiences may be different from yours or theirs might be distorted. If, after careful consideration, you still feel the need to act, direct your concerns to the *specific actions* of the perpetrator—not to the individual personality or the group to which he or she belongs.

Don't Rehearse It

Don't obsessively commiserate with your "buddies." Every time you tell your story to others, the perceived offense grows larger and more insidious. Avoid the tendency to recall and recount past incidents. That which happened in the past, and has been dealt with, should remain in the past. Don't dredge up historical issues—look forward. Your emotional tie-in to the issue deepens with every reiteration of the saga, and you run the risk of "donating" your emotionally laden baggage to innocent bystanders who will, after time and repetition, begin to remember this experience as if it were their own.

Try to Disperse It

If you are going to succeed in life, you may have to forgive—if not forget—others' transgressions caused by insensitivity or ignorance. Holding on to your anger will only block your opportunities because you will begin to see discrimination where none exists and you will behave accordingly. This may cause others to see you as angry and hostile, with a chip on your shoulder. Just as essential as it is to effectively internalize your feelings and reactions, so is it essential to know how to make an effective response, if you decide that is the best action to take. Trust yourself to give feedback and trust others to take feedback. Let's look at some external principles of what to do and what to say.

THE EXTERNAL PRINCIPLES

• *Initially assume that the person is well-intentioned, but uninformed or unaware of the effects of his or her remarks or behavior. Allow the person to "save face."* It's often useful to preface a response by saying, "You probably didn't mean anything negative just now, but I'd like to clarify what you said" or "I felt really uncomfortable when you said that" or "I'd prefer that you didn't use that expression." Waheed could have said this when others referred to him as an Indian instead of a Pakistani. He could have also said that, although he is proud of being a Pakistani, he doesn't like being identified only by his nationality (even if it's "the Pakistani" instead of "the Indian"); he's also a co-worker and an engineer. Being called by his nationality, instead of by his name, categorizes him as an outsider.

Mike, too, could have explained to his boss why he felt uncomfortable with his remarks about the way Latinos dress or the typical physical characteristics of a Latina. Mike could, of course, have prefaced his remarks by *not blaming or labeling* his boss about his motives or attitudes.

The key is to state the facts and your feelings assertively. Be sure to describe the situation and the effects the statement or behavior had on you and the group to which you belong. Do not attack the other person but simply inform him or her and assume that the comments were made innocently. Lori, Pam, and Jack handled their situations successfully because they consciously assumed that people were well intentioned but unaware of the effects of their remarks or behavior. This mindset was the catalyst for their success stories.

In Lois and Jean's case, they needed to forgo their assumption of hostility on the part of "all men." They needed to educate their bosses on the new realities of the workplace, as women's role increases in numbers and importance.

• *Ask questions to clarify intent.* Fred could have asked his staff questions to determine why they weren't working productively. Were they unclear about objectives or deadlines? Did they have a special loyalty to the previous boss?

Waheed could have asked, "Do you really think that I support terrorism because I follow the faith of Islam?"

Lori's success story showed her asking for help in dealing with "intent." She learned not to see her colleagues' actions as exclusionary or sexist. She asked for help on being more assertive and having her ideas acknowledged. Pam Cortez, too, asked a question to clarify her boss's remark about not knowing any other Latinos who could complete a particular project. She helped educate her boss by assuming not hostility on his part, just insensitivity or lack of knowledge. "How many Hispanics or Latinos do you know?" she asked directly and not sarcastically. She checked her baggage, listened respectfully, and tried to clarify for both of them what was meant and why. Tricia checked her assumptions about the boss's "compliments," first with other workers and then directly with her boss.

Another approach would be to ask a "confirming" question when you think you understand what the speaker has just said and why he or she said it. A "confirming" question might be, "Did you think Latinos couldn't do this project because you never knew one who could?" as Pam could have asked. Confirming or paraphrasing in your own words serves four purposes:

1. It ensures that the speaker and listener are working with the same information.
2. It helps the listener focus on what the speaker is saying instead of straying into his or her own thoughts or reveries.
3. It proves to the speaker that you have listened carefully because you can skillfully paraphrase his or her "significant utterances." People want to feel that what they are saying is important.
4. The speaker gains fresh insight into the crux of the statement when it is made in someone else's words. It helps the speaker understand insensitivities on his or her part and how the remarks might have been misconstrued or misunderstood.

• *Suggest that statements or behaviors may be a reflection of a societal stereotype.* Mike could have mentioned that many people assume that all Latinos like bright colors, but that is a stereotype. While there may be a cultural tendency—on the part of some—to favor bright colors, not all Latinos adhere to this. Moreover, he could have pointed out that lots of European-Americans like bright colors as well: Marimekko, a Scandinavian fabric company whose products are sold throughout the United States, uses bright, primary colors in most of its fabrics.

Waheed could have discussed stereotypes about people who follow Islamic traditions and how the stereotypes differ from reality.

• *Don't play the "heavy" by being negative or accusatory. Instead, adopt a respectful demeanor. Under certain circumstances, you may even choose to ignore the behaviors and comments.* Certain organizational realities might restrict your response. If the person making the insensitive comments is your immediate boss and the relationship is not good, you might think twice about giving voice to your reactions. You may choose to "ignore it." But this decision should be a conscious choice that you've made after analyzing all the alternatives. You may choose not to speak because you feel that the potential consequence of the discussion may be worse than the comments made.

The lesson here is to be aware of—and weigh—*the consequences* of the judgments you make and of your behaviors based on those judgments. Weigh everything in terms of *your* long-term opportunities for success.

Jack, the black attorney, was successful in his relations with his peers because he tested what could be seen as exclusionary behavior.

He made the effort to make others comfortable with *him*. Lori, the only woman in her group, decided to deal in a positive way with her annoyance about the constant "sports" talk in the office. She decided to "join them, not fight them." She was also assertive in telling the men how she felt about their sexual innuendoes and asked them to "quit it." She noted that "it was the lightness of my style that seemed to work." Pam respectfully asked her boss, whose remarks certainly could have been taken as stereotypical, for clarification of his meaning and intent. Instead of jumping into an accusatory response, she made him aware of his insensitivity and lack of information. And Tricia, after doing a reality check with other employees, respectfully told her boss, "Please stop that behavior because it makes me uncomfortable." And her feedback to her boss worked.

One of the most elusive commodities between people of the dominant culture and "others" is respect. A perceived lack of respect can affect communication to the point that cynicism frequently takes over. If someone says to you that your report or project is good, you can perceive a negative slant to every phrase uttered or second-guess every word of praise, as Tricia first did. You can decide that you're being patronized. Or you can accept the positive feedback as real, check your cynicism, and, as Pam, the Latina, did, clarify what the speaker is saying.

Please understand that we are not advocating or expecting that you have an overnight epiphany and gain immediate understanding of or respect for the other person, especially if you feel that he or she has not shown respect for you. Your respect for someone is an attitude, and attitudes sometimes are hard to change. But we're talking success now, and if you can't change your attitude, at least try to *behave* in a respectful manner.

Respect is circular. As you show respect, in many cases others will pick up that behavior and react similarly. Listening carefully is one measure of respect; watching your nonverbal communication is another. A calm, nonsarcastic tone, with a neutral facial expression, does wonders when you want to convey "respect" for the other person.

Pam, Jack, Lori, and Tricia could have certainly assumed racism and sexism on the part of their co-workers or bosses. But they made a choice to forgo or check out those assumptions, and respect and deal with people "where they are now." All four took the initiative to overcome mutual discomfort, clarify "hostile" remarks or actions, and learn to work successfully with others. They did this by calmly asserting themselves without making their co-workers or bosses feel " 'put down." *By not playing the hurt and angry "victim," they helped their own careers.*

SUMMARY

STRATEGY 1: CHECK YOUR BAGGAGE

1. Don't assume hostility when it may not be there just because of bad experiences you or others (whose baggage you have borrowed!) have had.
2. Act appropriately (in your own interests) when someone may be insensitive but his or her long-term behavior and motives are not necessarily hostile. Clarify intent, educate the person, and let the other person "save face."

STRATEGY 

CALL OUT THE CAVALRY

You Need All the Help You Can Get!

After years of preparation and study, Max is ready for his entrance into the new world. He has traveled far and has allowed his mind to conjure up all sorts of scenarios of what that new world will be like. In every scene, he envisions he is welcomed, appreciated, and excited to be there among his new associates.

Unfortunately, upon his arrival he is welcomed not with open arms but with skepticism. His difference is not appreciated, but ridiculed. People are not excited to be with him-; rather, they are either angry at his presence or afraid of him. Max is bewildered and confused. As hard as he tries to "win friends and influence people," he is always treated distantly.

Sure, there are obvious physical differences between him and his newfound associates, but they look strange to him, too. Upon personal introspection, Max comes to believe that he is isolated because he is different. Their language, while it sounds familiar, is different. Their customs, while reminiscent of what he has studied, are not his customs. He feels awkward, frustrated, anxious, and tense. He is sure that this discomfort is evident to his associates, too, and concludes that he must work harder to "fit in."

Alas, he cannot quite find the right niche. He decides to leave and go back to where he came from. The opportunity for Max and his associates to learn from each other is lost. Max concludes that "they" were not ready for him.

The foregoing scenario could very well be a scene from Steven Spielberg's film *E.T.—The Extra-Terrestrial*. Unfortunately, this is an all-too-common scene from the workplace. New and "different" workers study and prepare for years to enter the workplace, only to be rebuked, or seemingly rebuked, upon their arrival. It is not important to determine who is to blame. What *is* important for us to determine is how Max, and thousands like him, can fit in.

What is Max's responsibility in such a situation? How could he have "made" it? Remember, in our previous chapter we discovered that not everyone is hostile in the new world. Just as E.T. found Elliot, Max needs to find his Elliot—or, more likely, his multiple Elliots. Consider Mario Vasquez, a Latino-American project director in a large food conglomerate. Mario tells us, "No one can make it on his own. You need other people to become a success." Leila Baretta, a fifty-year-old bank vice president who is a lesbian, says, "You need everyone around you to want you to succeed—from your secretary to the president of the company." Both agree: A key to success in any organization is building a strong network of relationships, people who will actively help you on your way to success.

Of course, you have to be proficient at the critical elements of your job. However, the hallways of corporate America are littered with the bodies of talented, competent workers. The sad news is that most of them stay stuck in a job without advancing and without realizing their full potential. Granted they have mastered their job, but they have not mastered how to maneuver through the corporate and organizational maze. Too many people think their good work should speak for itself—that management will always reward good work. As a prominent African-American executive in the computer industry says, WAKE UP! That is NOT the way it works.

With this strategy, "Call Out the Cavalry," we will explore how to develop those critical relationships that will separate you from the rest of the pack. We will focus on developing relationships with people on *many* different levels within your organization.

How do you know if others are going to help you? Do they wear a sign that so indicates? If only it were that obvious!

What if you select the wrong person to show you the ropes? At least you'll know whom not to depend on the next time. E.T. didn't find Elliot right away, and Elliot kept his "friendship" with and assistance to E.T. secret for a while. Once Elliot openly revealed his relationship with E.T., others began to join in the circle of friends. This can happen in the workplace, too. We must seek out someone who wants—or is, at least, willing—to help. He or she, in turn, will gradually bring additional people to the circle.

A mentor, who is a power broker or a top decision maker, may be essential to propel you, to promote or sponsor you within the organization's inner sanctum. Peers with special information are also critical in your network because they can help you get the resources you need to be a star. The support staff is crucial in making sure your work gets done on time and is accurate; they are the backbone of every organization because they are a significant source of information, which, in turn, is power.

You need friends and supporters all over the organization—high and low. A speechwriter in an insurance company who uses a wheelchair states: "I make friends all over the organization. Some people talk only to important people. I speak to everyone. You don't know who or where that person will be in 10 or 15 years."

Remember, networking, building relationships, being mentored and coached—all these are essential for *anyone* to be successful. But if you are the "other," the task is harder and may even seem impossible. But if you want to move from the outside in, the effort is worth it.

Following are some real-life workplace scenarios in which people did *not* "call out the cavalry," and then some suggestions for how they could have gotten help from other people in their workplace quest for success.

SCENES FROM THE WORKPLACE

"MY CULTURE IS A BARRIER TO THE AMERICAN WORKPLACE"

Karen Lamm, a Chinese-American, came to the United States from Hong Kong when she was six years old. She is now a financial systems analyst for a large mutual fund. She is assigned by her department head to coordinate work on two projects because of her superb analytic skills. Her new assignment involves supervising four analysts—three men and one woman—with whom she formerly worked as equals. Her relationship with them is cordial, but distant.

She sees this opportunity as a means to demonstrate her abilities as a manager. She wants to overcome the stereotype that describes Asian-Americans as good technicians but weak managers.

She is concerned that the four people she supervises are not as thorough with their projects as she is. She is also aware that they are quite lax about their deadlines.

At her first meeting with them as their supervisor, she tells them of her high expectations for the project and her need for their cooperation. Because they are former co-workers, she is hesitant to give them specific direction on procedures to accomplish the project. She tries not to be too firm with them about their being thorough and punctual for fear of insulting them, but she does show her concern about these issues. To her dismay, at the end of the meeting, she overhears one worker say to another, "Karen sure is hard to read. Can you tell what she's really thinking?"

The work that is submitted in the next four months is well below Karen's standards and disappointing to her boss, John Norris, as well. Karen is embarrassed to tell John about her concerns but instead assures him that it will take only a little longer to get her unit into shape.

She then resolves to make up for the slack performance of others and takes her staff's work home several nights a week to improve upon it. But the stress begins to get her down. She feels humiliated because it seems that the staff doesn't respect her authority, and her boss sees her as inadequate. She is at a loss as to what to do or to whom to turn. And she had such great hopes when she began her new assignment. Karen needs help—and fast!

What Should Karen Have Done?

Karen should have done the following:

1. Before accepting this supervisory position, Karen should have reviewed her assets and deficits in terms of managing others and, most important, her relationship with other staff members—her boss as well as those she would be supervising. This is important because it is always awkward to supervise former peers, even when the prior relationship was a good one.
2. A priority for Karen should have been enlisting her boss, John, as an ally. She should have told him of her concerns about working with former peers and her desire to excel as a manager. Asking advice and help from her boss and confiding to him her objectives and concerns could be a positive step in gaining his support as she begins her new assignment. She should have told him of her plans to get some additional supervisory training and expressed confidence in herself while asking for his advice. Many people are flattered that you value and want their expertise, as long as you appear to be a competent person yourself.
3. Karen should have reflected on the cultural tendencies of her Asian-American background that might affect her interpersonal style. She, like many traditional Asian-Americans, is a reserved person, and this might prove to be a deficit in supervision. Her indirect style can be misinterpreted and perceived as weakness, uncertainty, or even lack of interest. Karen should have been very specific in describing her expectations to her staff. In addition, she may have related to her supervisor as she would to an authority figure in her own family instead of as a helpful colleague.
4. To ensure that she and her staff understood each other, Karen should have talked to them frequently to know what they were thinking. This would have given Karen a chance to clarify or correct any misunderstandings or misperceptions on her part or the staff's.

   Getting support from her staff was essential. They could have provided valuable information on staff concerns. Also, more frequent and frank interactions between Karen and her staff could have revealed Karen's "human side," which would have invited more cooperation from her staff.

5. Karen should have sought a working relationship with other supervisors on her level. Doing this would be another "stretch" for her in getting additional support and information. It is important to hear "shared stories" from others about how to be an effective supervisor and elicit employees' maximum productivity.
6. Karen should join an organization of Asian-American managers to discuss ways of assuming a more assertive mode of communication and building strong team relationships. She should seek support in overcoming her discomfort in adopting a more direct and clear leadership style. She should learn how others with her background adapted. At some point, Karen will have to decide how or whether she can adapt or change her cultural style.

What Might Karen Have Said to Her Boss?

Karen might have said the following to her boss: "John, I am really pleased at having this opportunity to supervise this unit, and I appreciate your confidence in selecting me. I know I will meet your expectations, but along the way I would like—and welcome—any advice you might have for me. If convenient, I'd like to stop by weekly to discuss our joint expectations and some of the pitfalls to avoid. I am especially concerned about supervising some of the people I used to work with. I know I might have to modify some of my interpersonal style, but I can accept that challenge—especially if I know I can count on your support."

THE "LONE RIDER"

Claudia Washington, an African-American, is an eleven-year veteran at a major telecommunications company. As a recent graduate of a state university MBA program (accomplished at night over a period of five years), Claudia is anxious about career development. Claudia has always believed that the organization appreciated hard work, dedication, long hours, quality performance, and a sense of personal sacrifice. As a single parent of two school-age children, Claudia often wonders how she accomplished so much with so many pressures and so many personal demands on her time.

Most of Claudia's co-workers describe her as independent and practical. Known to make quick decisions, she has lived by the motto "Occasionally wrong, but never in doubt." Claudia believes that this hard-nosed, aggressive, quick-decision-making style has made it possible for her to survive and overcome obstacle after obstacle on her career path. She also thinks these strengths will pay dividends when promotion time comes.

In meetings, Claudia tends to speak forcefully, use many ten-dollar words (some of which send people to their *Webster's*), and stare people down with intimidating looks.

For the past three years, Claudia has constantly performed above expectations, and her performance appraisals reflect those accomplishments. Risk taking has been her hallmark recently, and the department has greatly benefited from her decisions. But Claudia is not without her detractors. Some co-workers see her as too tough and domineering. Claudia quickly dismisses these criticisms as petty jealousy.

Last month, Claudia was appointed to an existing quality improvement team. She immediately made several "suggestions" on how the team should be working. Not unaccustomed to controversy and conflict, Claudia—with intimidating glares—quickly criticized the team for its "childish" behavior. This certainly did not win Claudia favor with the team.

Claudia, however, was undaunted. The next day she went to senior management to express concern about the "dysfunctional" behavior of the group and the apparent lack of leadership demonstrated by the team leader. Furthermore, Claudia indicated that a change in leadership might be in order if management wanted to maximize the efforts of the team. And who would be the new leader? Claudia, of course!

Several months pass and Claudia does not receive any promotion or extra assignments. She laments that others less qualified than she have been promoted and are serving on other interdepartmental teams. Thoroughly confused and frustrated, Claudia contemplates either resigning from the organization or mentally "quitting and staying." After all, Claudia surmises, mediocrity seems to be what the company, or at least the boss, wants and promotes. So why work so hard? "Besides, being a black woman, I should have known I didn't stand a chance here."

What Should Claudia Have Done?

Claudia should have done the following:

1. Claudia should have realized that she couldn't make it alone; she had to develop relationships with others in the workplace. Al-

though many of her activities could be—and, in fact, were—done alone, she couldn't advance within the organization without support.

2. Claudia had to recognize the importance of being a team player. When given the opportunity to serve on an important team—the quality improvement team—she should have realized that one of her first goals was to be accepted, liked, and admired for her team skills by the other team members. Instead, she came in and criticized the group, directly and to the boss.
3. Claudia should have started her activities in the group by observing, then making nonjudgmental observations on how the process might be improved, subtly directing the conversation in constructive ways by asking questions for clarification, and, finally, after a reasonable period of time, offering suggestions for improvement. This way she would be seen as showing leadership potential within the group.
4. Claudia should not have criticized the group by name calling (accusing others of "childish behavior"), nor should she have used nonverbal admonitions like staring people down with intimidating glares. Instead of seeing herself as a judge of others, she should have seen herself as someone who could help them to function better.
5. Claudia should have asked her boss how she could be helpful to the group. Obviously, he recognized her talents by appointing her to the quality improvement team in the first place. Perhaps the boss could give her feedback on how her forceful, "fast" manner could be applied in a way that wouldn't antagonize or seem judgmental to others.
6. If Claudia had sought out one or more mentors or sponsors within the organization, they could have given her inside information and guidance. More important, they could have recommended Claudia for a position and spoken on her behalf if she had developed a positive relationship with them over time.
7. Claudia should have questioned herself about whether she is too suspicious of others. Maybe her experiences have made her gun-shy in developing relationships. She should seek out those who might be friendly and helpful to her and judge each person individ-

ually, based on their specific actions toward her. Claudia needs to check her baggage—her assumptions of racism and sexism! If she doesn't, it will be hard for her to build relationships.

What Might Claudia Have Said to the Quality Improvement Team Leader?

Claudia might have said the following: "I am delighted that I was asked to be on the quality improvement team. Since it's been in operation for some time, I'd appreciate your bringing me up to date on what's happened so far. I'm full of ideas and I know I have a tendency to jump—some might say barge—right in. I'm trying to correct that tendency and I'd appreciate your feedback at any time because I would like to be an asset to the group and really look forward to working with you and the other members of the team."

What Might Claudia Have Said to Her Boss?

Claudia might have said the following: "Thanks for putting me on the quality improvement team. I've been to a few meetings and think I can be of help, but I don't want to move in too fast. You know the work I've already done for the company. How do you see me using my skills optimally, without stepping on other committee members' toes? I'd like your help because I want to move up in the organization and see this as a chance to develop some real leadership skills as a team member."

Success Stories

Following are some examples of people who were successful through winning support from others, each in a different way.

"YOU HAVE TO REACH OUT"

Walter Lee is the manager of a branch office of a large brokerage firm located in an upscale suburban city. Walter, who is Chinese-American, explained, "It is rare for Asian-Americans to hold this kind of position in a non-Asian community. Most Asians in this field are in systems or finances in the corporate offices of large companies. They are rarely involved in the 'retail' part of the business, dealing directly with the public.

"Although I was a finance major as an undergraduate, I decided early that I wanted wide options in my career. I chose the company I'm with now, one of the largest, because one of the top people in the company—right next to the CEO—is Asian. I could tell from my initial interview that I could be valued as a person and not stereotyped into a 'typically Asian' position. I was told, 'Look at our company and see what you want to do and then go for it.' I looked at the annual reports of other companies, and saw no Asian faces or names. I knew that the Asian voice was silent. Even though this company didn't give me the highest offer, I knew that I could have a future here if I handled myself right.

"My success in this company has been due in large part to my networking—in a lot of different ways. It helps that I like to socialize. Soon after I started here, I initiated and organized social functions with the 100 or so entry-level management associates who started the management training program with me. These associates were later spread out all through the company, so I established contacts throughout the company early on.

"It helped that I was used to being surrounded by non-Asians. In high school, I was a quarterback on the football team. People would be surprised. They'd say, 'He's Asian. He can't throw the ball.' But I did. Of course, I'm very proud of being Asian, being Chinese-American, but I don't want to be seen as *only* Asian. I view myself as a person first. I'm seen as someone who feels comfortable with everyone, not just with Asians.

"It was helpful for me to get mentors who were not Asians. How did I do this? When I came into a new position, I'd phone someone on another level and say, 'I just joined the company (or the department) and I've heard a lot about you. Can I call you to talk about some ideas I have?' Most people were flattered. I was never turned down. Once I got to know someone, I'd call and ask, 'What do you think my next move should be in this situation?' or 'I have a problem here. Can I brainstorm some solutions with you?'

"Some people, especially Asians, don't do this. They don't feel entitled to ask for advice or they think they may be betrayed and seen as ineffective or weak if they ask for help or admit they have a problem.

I don't agree. I feel entitled to ask for help, and I have never been betrayed by anyone I turned to for advice.

"Asians—like everyone else—have to reach out and initiate relationships. Otherwise your options are limited."

"YOU CAN CATCH MORE FLIES WITH HONEY THAN VINEGAR"

Albert Kazinski, who emigrated from Poland twelve years earlier, is a department manager in one of a nationwide chain of nursing homes and rehabilitation centers. During his ten-year tenure, he has seen several facility directors come and go. But regardless of who the director was, he never felt that he was that person's equal. Albert is, you see, the head of the facility's maintenance department, which includes housekeeping and laundry services. Since he started in the job, he detected from his peers—other department heads—that he was not considered a professional. After all, they were responsible for nursing, finance, food, and administration. All *he* was responsible for was "cleaning the toilets." On several occasions during staff meetings, he was not just ignored but was told that his department was "full of uneducated ghetto hoods or illegal aliens."

Albert tells us, "I know my people aren't as educated as many of the other staff and that some of them are immigrants—all legal—but they work hard and take pride in their jobs.

"And frankly, they usually show more respect and care for the residents than do the so-called professionals whose job it is to take care of them.

"I felt continually isolated by the other department heads, but I wanted to break the ice. I noticed that during some of the staff meetings two of the people did not take part in the 'trashing' of my department. Outside the meetings, I began to reach out to these potential allies by chatting with them when I saw them in the halls. Finally, I confided in Pat, who seemed the friendliest, and told her how I felt in the meetings. Pat reminded me that I could 'catch more flies with honey than vinegar.' I was familiar with the expression but didn't quite see how I could apply it. Every day for a week Pat would ask me, 'Use any honey yet, Al?' I would just smile and say, 'I don't know what kind to buy.' One day, just before a staff meeting, I put together several bunches of fresh-cut flowers from my garden and gave them to the other department heads with a note. The note said, 'Thank you for all your support and professionalism. It makes me strive even harder to exceed our goals for the residents.' Well, the 'honey' worked! Everyone immediately started asking me questions about the flowers and the gardening. People were surprised and impressed about how much I knew about plants. Within a few weeks, I was greeted in a warm and friendly way whenever the other department heads saw me, and the negative comments about my staff stopped.

"I built relationships based on respect for my talents that reached beyond the job and into their lives. Later, when I spoke to Pat again, she applauded me for my wise use of 'honey.'

"Because of my improved working relationships, the top administrators at the nursing home began noticing me, and I was appointed to an advisory committee on maintenance for the entire chain. I hope this will lead into more opportunities for me within the chain."

"I MAKE PEOPLE FEEL COMFORTABLE WITH ME"

Pete Shiller is an elected public official who uses a wheelchair. He served as mayor of a medium-sized town and now holds a major position in a large county in the Northeast. "When I ran for mayor and then later for the county position, I was told 'You're crazy; you can't campaign actively enough in a wheelchair and, for those people who *do* meet you, they'll be sure that you can't do the job.'

"I disagreed. I felt that I could make people see my talents and not just my disability. I had been doing this since high school. I was a leading high school athlete and became a paraplegic at 17 as a result of a swimming accident. But I completed college and law school, and I even had an active law practice before I was elected to a local and then countywide office.

"The first key to being accepted is to demonstrate your expertise. Next is to make other people feel comfortable. Make them see that there really isn't so much of a difference between us. I go out of my way to find common ground with other people—sports or other interests—so that the focus isn't on my disability.

"I found that one way to make others feel comfortable is to explain to them what happened to me and what I can and cannot do. People are naturally curious and when they see you in a wheelchair, they don't know what to think. With a few explanations, my disability becomes 'matter of fact.'

"I make sure to involve all the people I work with in understanding—and feeling comfortable with—my limitations. Before I go to a public speaking engagement, I'll ask my secretary to find out if the building is accessible. I'm very clear about my needs, and I've found this makes others comfortable. If people are *too* solicitous, I'll say nonconfrontationally, 'Thanks, but I can take care of that myself.' I'm not defensive at all. I know that others just don't know what my abilities are. I've found that most people's hearts are in the right place, but you have to explain things to them. You can't do it in one day. You have to get to know each other. And I know that in most cases, *I* have to be the first one to take the initiative. And that's worked out very well for me. But I don't think I'm exceptional. Look at Franklin Delano Roosevelt; he led the 'free world' during World War II and did it all from a wheelchair! It's too bad he had to hide that fact. Hopefully, we've made some progress since then."

"I MAKE PEOPLE FEEL GOOD ABOUT THEMSELVES"

Barbara Cappolli is the senior vice president in the corporate department of a very traditional bank. Twenty years ago she never thought she'd make it this far. "My name ends with a vowel. In those days bias against Italian-Americans was common in many 'old-line' financial institutions, and women were usually pigeon-holed in 'ghettoized' departments like operations and personnel."

In addition to her ethnicity and sex, Barbara came from a working-class background and attended college at night. But she decided early: "I love the world of banking. And I'm going to try to be successful." She adds, "My working-class Italian background and being a woman—all seemed to be against me. When I started, I never imagined I'd get to the level I am now. I realized early on that I could be lost in my small department, so I decided to meet people in other areas of the bank. Since my job limited my access, I became very active in special activities. I joined the charity committee. I volunteered to write a column for the bank newsletter. I became the bank representative for the Christmas Club investment program. In each activity, I met people from different areas of the bank and discovered it was crucial that you be liked by everyone or almost everyone. I pride myself on developing a real sense of loyalty from people I've worked with.

"What else did I learn from my activities? I found out about jobs I'd never even heard of before. I became friendly with people throughout the bank who later supported me or sponsored me for promotions. People working *for* me also became loyal supporters.

"I asked people for help in doing what they excelled at. For example, one of the men on the investment committee was an excellent speaker. I asked him, 'How do you make your presentations so exciting? What can you teach me so that I can be good at it, too?' Not only did I flatter this man, who became a sponsor for me at the bank, but I learned his skill and became known throughout the bank as someone to be called on to make a strong presentation.

"What worked for me is to be complimentary—about something I really admire—and to show a human side, without being too personal. I was shy at first, but found that in working on small committees, I could get to know other people in an easy, informal way. Many of these people became real friends. We weren't in a competitive situation on a daily basis, so it may have been easier."

Barbara says that one of her ground rules for success is "Try to make others feel good about themselves. Be a good listener and be complimentary—about something real. Don't ever be a phony—you'll be spotted in a minute."

Barbara got to know many people at work—many of whom helped her career—through her "extra" activities at the bank and through "making others feel good."

Principles of Calling out the Cavalry

The Importance of Building Relationships

The theme of this strategy is that in order for you to do well, people throughout the organization (and outside the organization, too!) have to like you, want you to succeed, and then actually help you. Your success as an "outsider" will usually be linked to your relationships as much as it is to your work.

You may say, "But the real question is, what do I have to do to get others in the organization to like me, to include me in the informal network? How do I get a mentor or someone else to help me? Should I seek out someone or should I let others seek me out?" It is hard enough for people in the dominant culture to develop relationships, but if you're an outsider the barriers may seem even more formidable.

Excuses

First, let's look at some excuses you might have for *not* taking the initiative in seeking others out.

- "I'm uncomfortable about pushing myself onto other people."
- "I never know what to say around the water cooler."
- "I feel that others are uncomfortable around me; they never know what to say."
- "In my culture, you never approach someone first unless you are the boss or the authority."
- "I'm afraid women will think I'm coming on to them if I act friendly."
- "Maybe I'll be accused of sexual harassment."
- "I'm shy and I want to spend any free time with my family. And I don't like golf."
- "Isn't merit the key to success? Shouldn't I be rewarded because I do a great job, not because I'm good at socializing?"

So here's the dilemma. Now you know that whom you know is important—and that's on every level. Yes, it's essential. We're talking "face time": meeting in person with your boss, the boss's boss, your staff (subordinates, if any), your peers—getting to know them on a personal level, being seen with them, taking initiatives in social situations or informal encounters.

Sounds like good advice. But you say that you just can't do it. A Latino first-line supervisor whose career is stalled said, "I'm just not comfortable making the first move. It's part of our religion. You're taught that things will come your way; don't take risks." An Asian-American engineer said, "Our culture teaches us to stay in the background. We don't want to stand out."

The issue of socializing to gain acceptance and friendship at work may be difficult for many, whatever the group to which they belong. But talk to every successful "outsider" who has made it. Each will invariably say that it's a tremendous challenge to get "out of yourself," to give up your reserve and gain the confidence to fight your way in. It's always easier to stay with your "own people," but it's essential to expand the range of people you know. Outsiders who have made it say they will not be intimidated and threatened and "play the victim."

Use the Acronym SAME as a Tool

We suggest that the word *SAME* is truly an acronym for building successful relationships. The acronym stands for the following:

S Socialize.
A Acknowledge.
M Maximize mutual interests.
E Empathize.

Ever notice that we tend to feel comfortable around those who are the same as we? There is a certain ease of conversation, a genuineness, a comradeship. Embodied in the word *SAME* are the strategies for becoming more widely liked and appreciated within the organization. Let's examine this more closely and see if the elements of the acronym SAME can paradoxically be used to feel more comfortable with people who do not seem to be the same as you—at least not at first sight.

S in SAME Is for Socialize

Recognize that your cultural background may have taught you *not* to take the initiative in relationships. Yes, you may be uncomfortable in taking the first step in conversations or in any social interactions. You may do better when others approach you first. That's fine, but what if they *don't* approach you? To get ahead in any organization—business or social—you have to *stretch your comfort level by initiating contact with others*.

During the 1990s, there was a plethora of movies concerning extraterrestrial life—the ultimate outsiders. The singular message of these films was that if you wanted a profitable relationship with someone different from yourself, you had to be the one to reach out and establish it. Someone had to begin the process of socializing. Someone had to make contact. How do successful people of difference reach out and make contact? Here are some tips to consider for socializing:

1. Recognize your cultural taboos. In the business culture of the United States, it is not considered impolite or rude to approach someone first. Also, the attitude toward authority is different here from what it is in many other traditional societies. In most cases, it is considered acceptable for employees to approach their supervisor first. The social distance between employees and supervisors is just not as great as in many Latino or Asian countries.

   Remember, if you want someone to accept you, you must first accept yourself. Know who you are; know what you "bring to the party," know what barriers you have to overcome from your own background.

2. Many African-Americans say that they have a "sixth sense" about those in the dominant culture. They believe that they "know" when someone will be disapproving or condescending to them. That sixth sense notwithstanding, there is an inherent danger in acting or not acting because of some anticipated negative behavior from others. This will very much limit your exposure to others who could be of help to you in the future or even be a friend! So try to assume the best about each individual—until you have *personal* experiences that cause you to be distrustful. Your "sixth sense" may be helpful, but it's not always accurate because you may be carrying too much "baggage."

   Jackie Gorman, the only black female executive in a large pharmaceuticals company, was not invited to lunches with other executives. "Subtle exclusion," she called it. But since she knew that socializing is a must, when she saw all the other senior executives show up at the cafeteria at 11:50 a.m., she showed up, too. Of course, they included her at their table. "I can win at their game if I'm willing to play, and I am!" she said.

   A Mexican-American woman senior manager at a leading

magazine and publishing organization said, "I have lunch with important people, and I usually initiate it. For instance, I called the new CEO to have breakfast with him and offered to explain anything he wanted to know about the company or my projects. He was delighted. Usually, Latinos are not comfortable doing this, but I realized that what counts in an organization like mine is seeing people and being remembered. Some Latinos, especially women, usually have problems in taking the first step. But this attitude is hurtful to you. If you're committed to your success, you will take the time and effort for socializing. Force yourself, because how much time you are in the informal network and seeing people is what counts. You must make time for this. People will remember you."

3. Practice, practice, practice. At first you might feel uncomfortable, awkward, or even foolish. The good news is that it will get easier for you. Yes, sometimes you won't get a response back or worse, an unpleasant response after you have taken a risk and made yourself vulnerable. The person you approach may be rude or seem uninterested. But not everyone will, and not all the time. *We guarantee it.* Some of the time you will get a positive response when you reach out. Most people overcome shyness when they practice and get a positive response. You are not doomed to shyness. It is not your fate. Success is!

   A senior executive female attorney said, "I learned to 'infiltrate—not integrate' different social groups at work. I don't come in as a woman, but as a person. That's what I mean about infiltrating, not integrating. I try to have an invisible approach. I did everything to fit in when I first came to my company. I decided very early in my career that *I* wanted to be the person everyone knows, and I still work hard at this. I have a huge Rolodex full of contacts."

4. Don't reject overtures from others. Another side of socializing and building relationships is responding to an approach from others. Don't rebuke it no matter how skeptical you are. Respond to overtures. Don't automatically be suspicious. A successful African-American manager said, "When someone extends their hand to shake, do you first look to see if it's clean? " If your boss, co-worker, or subordinate makes an attempt to reach out to you—to invite you to lunch or share in some homemade cookies or ask you to play golf—take a chance.

Maybe your first impression of that person was that he or she was phony, patronizing, maybe even subtly racist. But you might have been mistaken. Accept that person until you are proven wrong. Remember our first strategy: *Don't assume that everyone is hostile*. Don't always question motives. Take a chance. Be a risk taker.

As the "other," it is *always* your responsibility to make people comfortable. Just as you have a problem with discomfort, others may be uncomfortable with you. Many people have not had the opportunity to work closely with a person who has a disability or someone who is Asian-American, African-American, Latino, or an immigrant who speaks English with an accent. Such people may feel timid or insecure in trying to find common ground. They may be afraid they'll say the wrong thing and offend you. So *you* have to find the common ground and make people feel at ease with *you*.

Remember the black attorney in the preceding chapter who put golf mementos on his desk as a conversation starter? Remember the public official who is a wheelchair user and his ability to put people at ease by explaining what happened to him?

A in SAME Is for Acknowledge

People enjoy talking about themselves. It's true. Give people the opportunity to wax eloquent about what they are most proud of in their lives. Hearing others talk about themselves gives you great insight into what they perceive to be important and provides factual data for you to "hook into" when you begin the process of demonstrating your *sameness* with them. To do this, don't worry about seeming only "interested" but not "interesting." You will get your chance to delve into your background later.

A good opener for a conversation may be, "Tell me about yourself."

At first, let the other person do the talking while you actively listen. Make mental notes of the things the other person sees as important. Then when you get back to your office, create some notes or a small file card on that person and record what you heard. Don't rely on your memory to recall important personal data later—you may not have it accessible. Write it down, store it, recall it.

Once you have identified several personal or business accomplishments, select one to get the person to expand upon it. You do not have to be knowledgeable about the subject—all you need do is demonstrate inquisitiveness and leave the rest to the other person. You might ask, "That has always fascinated me. How did you first get involved?" Or, "I have no experience with that, but I have always been intrigued by it. Were there any obstacles you had to overcome to be successful at this?" People like to tell how they identified and overcame obstacles.

Always concentrate on the other person, not on yourself. Compliment the person on something you've noticed about his or her work. Respond to something said with, "Yes, I agree that it's a good idea. Tell me more about it."

Smile and make eye contact. Say hello and nod to people as you pass them in the hallways. This conveys friendliness, and as a consequence others may feel more comfortable approaching you. If you look uncomfortable, others will feel uncomfortable with you.

One strategy of acknowledging others is often overlooked. If anyone—your boss, peer, subordinate—is active in community organizations or has a favorite charity and invites you to one of the functions, *go*. Yes, the "rubber chicken" dinner may be boring, but you have acknowledged and validated the person who invited you and he or she will be grateful and aware of your loyalty.

A Korean-American writer in a software company advised, "Be conscious of others' needs. Keep your eyes open. See what you can do to help. Someone you help today may help you tomorrow."

Don't overlook subordinates in acknowledging accomplishments. Make your subordinates feel part of your objectives by letting them know the specific importance of their work to the organization and to *you*. Their loyalty is a *must* if you are going to make it. And acknowledging their real accomplishments is an important strategy.

M in SAME Is for Maximize Mutual Interest

Once a conversation has been started and a rapport established, establish the third item in the *SAME* model, maximize mutual interests. These mutual interests could range from personal family issues to educational background to business projects. Seize every opportunity to explore that common interest with the other person. Showing a relevant news article or any special information is a way of developing a common interest. The key here is to bring something to the relationship, so that the other person feels that he or she is benefiting from the relationship, too. In exploring mutual interests, you might even find that you will learn something new or that, in your networking, you know of someone else who has the same interest. Take that opportunity to bring those parties together. You could make a significant connection for someone else who will not forget that favor.

But what if you don't like to play golf or meet after work for a drink? You'd rather just be with your own family. *The choice is yours.* If you refuse an invitation or an overture to socialize, the opportunity may not come again. People may invite you once or twice, but more than twice is rare. Two refusals and you are seen as a loner or as someone who is antisocial—not open to friends or relationships with others of the dominant culture. Your refusals may affirm what some people perceive as the "unfriendliness" of people not part of the dominant culture. Sometimes those who are in the dominant culture say of the others, "They just want to stay together and not mix with us." This perception may be just a rationalization for those who want to be exclusive anyway or it may be a response to having their overtures being rejected by "the outsiders."

Developing and maximizing mutual interests may sometimes be a stretch for you. A middle manager in an advertising agency who uses a wheelchair goes regularly to golf games with his peers and bosses. No, he can't play, but he meets with his colleagues after the ninth hole or at the end of their game to drink or dine with them and discuss golf. He is one of them.

Maximizing mutual interests involves networking with members of your own group. It is essential to recognize the need for finding others in the organization like you and building a support network with them. It can be lonely and frustrating without the assistance of friends. People who are like you may have experienced the same types of situations and feelings that you have.

If there are others in your organization of the group you identify with, reach out to them. You may learn much from them about how things are done there. But most of all, you can find a commonality and emotional support that you need. But a word of caution: Do not always be seen with *only* members of your own group. People will assume that you don't want to integrate into the social fabric of the organization.

If you are the only member of your group in the organization, go outside for your contacts. Join an organization of members of your own group. It can be a general group such as a Business and Professional

Association for Women, or a more specific professional organization with members of your gender, racial, or ethnic group such as the National Association of Black Women Attorneys, the National Association of Black Accountants, the Society of Hispanic Engineers—there are countless such organizations out there. These organizations can not only give you psychological support so you don't feel isolated but can also provide coaching, counseling, and specific career help for making it in your organization or elsewhere.

If you find that the organization isn't meeting your goals, make a suggestion or assume leadership in making it into the kind of organization you would like. The most effective networking groups usually include a social component, as well as specific information for problem-solving issues, feedback on personal improvement, or specific career strategies.

Another important source of outside contacts is with general professional groups: associations of accountants, engineers, graphic artists, and so on. Become active in those groups so that you can learn generic information about your field as well as make contacts that may be useful in the present or future.

For listings of literally thousands of organizations in every conceivable category, ask the reference librarian at any public library for the three-volume reference *Encyclopedia of Associations*. Organizations are listed alphabetically and by subject matter, with addresses and phone numbers. It's impossible not to find an organization that will be a source of useful networking. And, of course, the Internet is a source of infinite information on how to contact people who share your interests.

The Letter E in SAME Stands for Empathize

The final issue to consider is empathy—putting yourself into another person's state of mind and emotion. It's not easy to get inside another's heart or head, but in seeking to build relationships with others, especially when you are not of the dominant culture, it is vitally important to establish and maintain empathy. Don't confuse empathy with sympathy. The difference is profound in its application. In establishing empathy with the other person, be sure to establish a common understanding of the matter in question. Do not allow your filters to alter the meaning of the other person's message. Look and listen for the feelings being described as well as the facts of the situation.

Be sure to pay attention to the subtleties of the situation, and ask for clarification if you are not sure what the other person means.

By using solid listening skills, you actively demonstrate your empathy with the situation of the other person. Empathy allows for a connection at a very basic level. It transcends the cognitive (knowledge) level and catapults us to the realm of the visceral—the gut feelings. Even if you do not fully comprehend the facts of the situation, you can and must identify with the feelings in play. To ignore the feelings is to reduce your chances of making that connection—a connection that will produce a different level of communication and potential commitment. Recognize that everyone—no matter how high the position or how different from you—has personal and professional issues that may cause concerns or problems. By showing an interest in someone's problems, you are empathizing and making an invaluable connection. Regardless of any differences, we all share the human condition.

Another method of demonstrating empathy is to be mindful of other people's time. Making reference to the fact that you do not want to take up too much of their time signals that you value their time and respect it. If you ask someone for ten minutes of time, at the end of those ten minutes wrap it up. If the other person wants to continue the discussion, fine. But you will have demonstrated respect for the person's time, and that thoughtfulness sends a positive message.

Finally, empathy is not something that is established during the first fifteen minutes of a meeting and then forgotten. You must reestablish empathy on a meeting-by-meeting basis. Never assume that the empathy established in a prior meeting has "staying power" and that it will automatically roll over to the next chance or planned encounter. You must continually reestablish it throughout every meeting. See the situation from the other person's point of view; walk that proverbial mile in the other person's "moccasins."

Conversation Tips

Here are some conversation tips to get you started in each of the above: *S*ocialize, *A*cknowledge, *M*aximize Mutual Interests, and *E*mpathize.

1. Find out about the people with whom you work. Do they have families? Hobbies? Some successful people keep a card for virtually everyone they meet. If you choose to do that, include the person's

interests and where you met. If he or she is interested in dogs, write that on the card. Or maybe it's gardening or camping, and certainly professional interests. But suppose you don't know or care about dogs, gardening, or whatever the interest. *Learn*—if the contact is important. An older technician working for a young boss went to the library to learn about dog breeding because that was his boss's hobby.

Some people may find this kind of information gathering too calculating a strategy, but the purpose of finding out about others' interests is simply to help make a connection to the other person and add to your conversational repertoire.

2. Take the initiative to walk over to someone who is standing alone at a company function or meeting. Remember that many people, from the secretary to the CEO, may feel insecure or ill at ease in a large setting. Everyone wants someone to talk to. Many people do not know how to begin. You must make the effort.
3. Learn how to start a conversation. Lesson one: Smile warmly, then introduce yourself. You might start with one of these openers:

- To senior executives whom you've never met, begin by introducing yourself and ask their name and department (if you don't know) or show that you do know who they are by referring to their position.
- Find a connection between you and the other person. Before talking about work, you may want to comment about where you are, the immediate surroundings (such as the decor of the room), the atmosphere, the food (if any), even the weather. Try to talk with energy, enthusiasm, direct eye contact, and a smile.

Follow up on anything the other person says. Usually, the conversation will turn into something about work, or you can turn the conversation that way after a while. You might ask the other person how long he or she has been at the company and mention how long you've been there; ask what he or she sees as the differences in the organization between the time they came to the organization and now. Ask about his or her job and where they worked before this organization. Are there any new initiatives or goals in their department? Where are they from originally (geographic location)?

Whenever possible, emphasize *sameness*. Make a connection between the other person and your circumstance—whether similar or slightly different. Tell what you did before this job, or where you live. *But don't speak for too long.*

Concentrate more on the other person and look interested. Everyone wants attention and acknowledgment. As indicated earlier, a classic conversation opener is simply, "Tell me about yourself." (And be prepared if someone asks you the same question.) Variations on this theme can, of course, be used successfully at any point in a conversation.

In exploring mutual interests—within your organization or without—you may not only discover specific career help but also expand your appreciation of different cultures and activities. This information may not only make you a better person, with a variety of interests, but also afford you the opportunity to meet people you would never have come into contact with in your usual routine. You never know where help will come from, and, in the meantime, you will have expanded your worldview.

SUMMARY

STRATEGY 2: CALL OUT THE CAVALRY

1. You can't "make it" in the workplace alone. Take the initiative to get help from everyone, on every level—your boss, your peers, your subordinates.
2. Being liked is as important as your work skills.
3. Because you are not a member of the dominant culture, it is *your* responsibility to make others feel comfortable with *you*.
4. You need to find mentors, preferably someone from your own group as well as someone from the dominant culture.
5. You must *practice* talking to everyone, so that you feel more and more comfortable doing so.
6. To form relationships with people at all levels of the organization, remember the SAME model: *S*ocialize, *A*cknowledge, *M*aximize Mutual Interests, and *E*mpathize.

STRATEGY 3

ACCENTUATE THE POSITIVE

What You Can Do to Maximize Your Value to Your Organization

When we talk about accentuating the positive, we are talking about emphasizing all your strengths—professional and personal. For starters, *you* have to believe in the positive nature of what you have to offer. If you don't accept or value who you are, no one else can or will. Ask yourself, "What do I have to offer? What are my unique talents, skills, abilities, and personal attributes that make me a valuable player? What are the special assets that I bring to the organization?"

We assume that you have the basic technical skills and knowledge for which you were hired. But as you probably realize, if you are not a member of the dominant group in your organization, you have to have something "extra." An Indian-American public health executive said, "You are constantly being judged. People expect more from you than from others. That's because many people assume that you are inefficient and incompetent. You have to be better than anyone else. And you won't be forgiven for a mistake—at least not as easily as someone else might be."

Once you have identified your core strengths, how do you parlay them into a successful outcome? Here are ten "extras" that will bring a bottom-line benefit to your organization and assist you in reaching that successful outcome.

Ten Extras to Maximize the Value of Your Core Strengths

1. *Keep up with the latest trends in your field and use your new skills.* No job or job skill remains static. Tasks, jobs, and technology are changing so rapidly that you must constantly be learning. For example, in many jobs you must, at a minimum, keep up to date on the latest computer capabilities. In addition, everyone—yes, *everyone*—has to communicate constantly with others in the organization and outside the organization, using the most up-to-date technology. An older man who had worked for many years as director of security for a large clothing chain was forced into early retirement because he didn't have the computer skills needed for sophisticated inventory control. He said, "I was only fifty-five years old and I didn't want to retire, so I spent six months studying computer technology specifically related to inventory control. Eventually, I was hired as a manager in the security department of a department store. With my previous background plus my new technical know-how, I was again employable."

You have to know how new technology will enhance your job, even if you are in a supposedly "soft" field—say, human resources. You can keep current on legal trends, benefits, and training techniques by being active in your professional organization, reading current journals, and "surfing the Net." As most are beginning to realize, the Internet has expanded informational access to a level previously unimaginable.

Every field also has peripherally related fields. Let's say you are a trainer in management skills. Don't just stick to the training area and wait for people to come to you. Learn about the bigger picture in your company and what some of the key issues are. Be a problem solver and troubleshooter. Learn about the new trends and challenges in your organization and related fields.

Build a variety of skills; start with an expansion of those you already have. Relate new knowledge and skills to what you already know. If you were the management trainer cited above, you should learn about and take courses in employment law so that you have the essential information to respond to most questions and know where to get the answers to the more arcane questions. Be aware of how new organizational structures and trends can affect human resources issues. Expand your horizons and skills.

Just having knowledge or skills isn't enough. You have to know how they can be applied in a specific way to your job or the job you hope to have. An immigrant Russian project manager advised, "Don't wait for instructions from your boss. Find important information yourself and develop a new proposal." People may see you in the same old rut or position. Design a new presentation format for clients using new computer graphics. Write a new procedures manual based on a personnel course you took.

2. *Take risks; make decisions*. Learn when it is essential to ask for permission and when you can simply go ahead and *move*. Virtually all career development specialists stress how crucial it is to be a risk taker to get ahead. Yet according to a national diversity survey conducted by one of this book's authors, Vincent Ford, for VISTAR Corporation, it was found that nonwhite men and women were far less likely than white men or women to take risks on the job.

These are the survey findings for the following statement: "I take risks on the job that will set me apart from the rest and advance my career."

Category	**% Agree**
Hispanic/Latino Men and Women	40
African-American Men and Women	50
Asian-American Men and Women	65
White Women	85
White Men	90

These findings clearly suggest that minority employees do not take risks to the same degree as their white counterparts. By asking you to take a risk, we are not suggesting that you do something equivalent to taking a red marker, drawing a dotted line around your neck, and giving your boss the axe to summarily chop it off. However, we do suggest that you take *calculated risks* that allow you to fully demonstrate your capabilities.

Taking risks, however small, may be difficult for members of some cultural groups who are used to traditional authority patterns of asking for permission or authority to take action. But people from Asian and Latino backgrounds, as well as many women, can have an advantage here. These groups tend to use participatory decision making. Thus, before making a decision—which may involve risk—they may be willing to seek input and support from many different sources. Receiving wide and expert input can insulate you from making a horrendous mistake. Therefore, the risk may be limited since you will have a broad basis of information and support for taking the risk.

Remember, however, that consensus decision making may be seen as negative in some organizations. It may be seen as a sign that you are afraid to do anything on your own—to take any risk without the backing of a "committee." Instead of being seen as a strength, it can be seen as a weakness. It is up to you to explain your rationale and make it clear to bosses what the advantages are of your special style. You have to reframe consensus building as a strength, not a weakness, in taking risks. Demonstrate that you have your own ideas and judgments and, if necessary, can act solely on your own. However, you believe that a participatory style usually works better. Of course, if you are a supervisor, you must make certain decisions alone, especially on evaluations of employees and resulting decisions, such as promotions or firings.

3. *Seek job assignments that are line positions directly related to the organization's bottom line.* Historically, business executives have come from sales, marketing, manufacturing, and finance. Over and over we've heard that organizations seek executives who have had bottom-line, operating responsibility—and results. Basically, you have to understand how the organization as a whole works. If you aspire to an executive position, you should be aware that you can't be seen as a narrow specialist. Jobs in customer relations, human resources, community relations, or communications may get you to the top of those departments.

But that's as far as you'll get! Staying in those areas may be fine for you, as far as you'd like to go, and match *your* goal. But be aware of the limitations of staying in certain positions if you want to move to the top echelon of your organization.

4. *Maximize your appearance*. Yes, this may sound superficial. But people make judgments about you in the first 30 seconds after meeting you, and often these judgments are based on appearance. This does not mean that you have to wear a "corporate uniform." But you do have to learn the parameters for "successful" dressing in your organization. Imaginative clothing may be rewarded in some organizations. Look around and see how upper-echelon people dress in your organization. A young mid-level female manager on a fast track in a financial consulting firm says, "I always dress for the next level."

Some women have said they are more successful when they wear dresses with a "feminine" flair than when they are in the classic navy blue conservative suit. Men may be seen either as trendsetters if they dress in the latest style or they may be seen as not conservative enough. Test out *your* organization. While you are on the way up, there is less "forgiveness" about the way you dress than after you've made it.

5. *Have a high energy level.* Show enthusiasm, humor, and a sense of excitement about work. Indicate that you like challenges. Show self-confidence, even if you have to fake it at first. A top-level woman attorney in a large securities firm offered this advice: "Many women are seen as methodical, hardworking grinds or drudges. I tell women to be more talkative and flamboyant. You have to tell jokes, be animated. I watched others in meetings who get noticed—that's what they do."

Be very reluctant to turn down a challenging assignment; you can always get help on it. But don't take the assignment if you really don't have the time to do it well. In such a case, explain your commitments and enthusiastically express your appreciation for being considered and tell the person to call on you again. In fact, when you are close to completing the large project taking so much of your current time, go back to the person who invited you to work on the project and indicate your current availability and interest.

As one successful Ghanaian-American joked, "Don't be afraid to work hard!"

She added, "You will be judged harder than others—you have to be better and work harder. That's a fact of life." Variations of this theme were repeated by many successful people.

6. *Be organized.* Know how to use your time well. Develop a "time management system"—with daily written "To-Do lists," long-term and short-term goals, and a daily calendar. A key skill is to constantly evaluate your priorities and make sure that you are spending most of your time on the most important tasks. Delegate whatever can be delegated to someone else, but follow up to make sure the work is done. If because of your cultural or group background you are not comfortable asking others for help or delegating responsibilities, you will have to learn to overcome this qualm. Otherwise, you will spend your time on inconsequential and unrewarded activities, like a computer manager who did her own word processing and printing because she could not delegate work to her assistant. Who would look worse here, the supervisor or the subordinate?

An important part of being organized is making time to acknowledge and return phone, fax, or e-mail messages, if only very briefly. Returning messages promptly adds to your reputation as a responsible professional.

7. *Remember to make your boss look good.* A Japanese-American human resource manager described how she made her boss look good at every opportunity. For example, if someone complimented her on her work, she would often manage to say, "My boss gave me the chance to spend time on this project and gave me his full support and encouragement all along the way." She explained: "In my culture, it is hard to take compliments. We usually deny the compliment altogether, but I've learned to accept the compliment by deflecting it and sharing credit with my boss."

A young advertising assistant enhanced her boss's presentation to a major client by designing some of the material with the latest computer graphics. Her boss took credit for the total presentation, although he thanked her in private for the design, which was not part of her assigned work. Remember to not just ask what your bosses can do for you, but also what you can do for them.

8. *Share information about your background.* Many successful people share such information after they have a good working relationship, especially with those in power and authority. People are often curious, but afraid to ask. You can be a "cultural mentor," but don't be seen *only* as a representative of your group. Your "group" identity should be seen as another in your long list of skills, abilities, and contributions to the company.

An Indian-American health care administrator often wears a sari to the office. If someone asks her about the sari or her background, she provides answers briefly and in a friendly way. "But," she said, "after a brief explanation and some information about my background, I channel the conversation to my professional role or a common work interest. That's what's really important. I keep my culture, but I don't let it totally define me."

When asked about her background, a Vietnamese immigrant described her family's struggle to become American and how they were a proud people who had overcome extraordinary circumstances to get to the United States. She was both surprised and delighted that others were interested in her experiences and that people began to seek her out, both professionally and socially.

9. *Perfect your speaking and writing skills.* Communication skills can't be emphasized enough. Just as important as computer skills nowadays, speaking and writing skills are essential because they often convey the first impression you make on someone either in person or by mail (including e-mail or any other form of communication). People whose first language is not English sometimes feel that this judgment is unfair. It may be. But they should know that *everyone* is judged on speaking and writing ability. Even *Mayflower*-descended white men are judged on their writing and presentation skills. If too many people ask you, "What? Can you repeat that, please?" or if your supervisor returns your report drafts with many corrections in syntax and spelling, realize that you need help and get it. The American Institute of Banking, a continuing education organization for the banking industry, offers a course called "Improving Your Accent." It is not a requirement anywhere. And it is illegal to discriminate against individuals because of their accents. But surely communicating clearly helps people on their way up. Career development requires a reality check. How successfully do you communicate?

10. *Recognize your background as a strength.* And what else do you have that's extra, in addition to the nine foregoing strengths? You have to believe that your cultural inheritance or your group membership is an advantage, that it has helped you succeed, that your experiences and values have given you an inner strength and have made you tenacious and wise about the world in a special way.

Many people who are outsiders have experienced discrimination and have survived painful episodes in their lives. Those who have "made it" will not be vanquished. They won't let others define their lives. The ability to see life as a challenge, to rise above barriers, is one of the most positive attributes and skills that one can have in the working world.

Almost all people of color have said that their heritage and their values have been a strength for them. A Latino elected official in a major city said, "I never forgot where I came from. My father told me, 'Always look back—it will give you strength.' My strong family ties and my community are a tremendous source of strength for me." A disabled manager who uses a wheelchair explained, "My ability to overcome barriers makes me feel like a winner. I feel I can do anything. I will let nothing stop me. My disability is just physical. So many people without physical disabilities have personality disabilities that keep them back." A Cambodian refugee described how her father often reminded her of her "tough heritage" and how hard it was for the family to escape from Cambodia. When she first started working, she often felt invisible and very shy, but she eventually overcame this by remembering her father's words. She said, "I recalled his words and they filled me with pride. I still felt shy inside, but my father's pride and his struggle echoed and resonated deep within me to give me the courage to be a success."

Use your background or your group membership as an advantage. Be open about your group identity. Help people in top positions realize that you can help *them*. Many companies want more diversity. It's good business.

Your cultural or group background can be a positive in your working relationships. Some African-Americans pride themselves on being direct. Define that directness as a strength for yourself and the corporation. Ask for what you want. Take initiative, take risks. Some African-Americans have used these skills just to survive adversity. Use those skills to move ahead.

For many Latinos, personal relationships have a very high value. This cultural characteristic can be a good basis for developing strong teamwork and inclusiveness, to foster a motivating work environment for co-workers and staff.

For Asian-Americans, modesty, pride, and a desire for harmony are important values. These may work to your self-interest, but not if they serve to put you down. These values can be used to emphasize teamwork and to share credit with your boss for *your* achievements. Making the boss—or others on your team—look good will be advantageous to you as well in the long run. A female executive at a large accounting firm stressed that many organizations are now realizing the importance of diversity in attracting clients. She said, "We find that many women clients want women to work on their accounts. Many of these clients were themselves passed over because they were women. Now that they have made it, they want to 'dig back.' That's why they insist on having women work on their accounts."

A media executive who is gay said that he thought being "out" about his sexual orientation has some advantages. "People act negatively to someone closed. They can sense when you're 'shut down' or not being honest. For me, being 'out' is part of the honest package with me. I think that others think: 'If he's telling me he's gay, he's going to be open and honest with me about other issues.' I set the standard of being open and honest. The worst thing in business is to have a secret agenda and for others to suspect you of this. The more straightforward you are, the easier it is to get down to business fast. The gay thing becomes secondary. Besides, everybody has to overcome something difficult. Knowing I'm gay has opened the door for people to open up to me. They'll say, 'I have a gay brother' or they tell me about something else in their lives."

If you have a disability, you can show that your disability is not a barrier but a motivator to succeed, an opportunity to show your tenaciousness and indefatigable spirit.

As an older worker, you can demonstrate your broad and wide-ranging experience, your judgment, and your familiarity with your organization. This experience can be of great value, especially if your company is in an expansion mode. Perhaps you've "been there, done that" in several departments while working with a variety of companies. You are an important resource and can offer that resource to others, as long as you are keeping up with current trends as well.

You must be the definer of what your culture or group identity can offer. Review all your strengths and see how they can be incorporated into the mainstream work norms of your organization.

Never deny your uniqueness and your group identity. To be realistic, it's almost impossible to do so successfully. You can deny it, but not hide it because everyone is usually aware of your group membership anyway. While this is true for most people, it is not the case for many gays and lesbians who do hide because they are worried about negative reactions if their sexual orientation is known. Unlike skin color, accent, or a physical disability, sexual orientation can be, and usually is, invisible.

You have to learn how to show pride in and acceptance of your group identity but at the same time not be totally defined by that group membership. For example, you may be an important contributor to your organization as a marketing expert; your group identity is an enhancer of that skill because you can reach out to new and diverse markets.

The key is to use all your strengths. Imagine for a moment that your technical skills and your group membership attributes are unique muscle groups in your body. Furthermore, let's imagine that you exercise faithfully—but only the right side of your body. It is safe to say you will look great, be "buff"—but from a profile position only. Unfortunately, if a danger were to approach you from the left side of your body you would be too weak to react with strength because the muscle groups on that side would have atrophied from non-use. If you use only your technical skills and never tap into your special cultural or group attributes—a key part of who you are—after a while that specialness will no longer be available for your use. You will have lost an important advantage.

It is imperative that you, as an employee of difference, identify and exercise all of your special attributes—that you accentuate *all* your positives.

Here are some workplace scenarios that will help you learn how to "accentuate your positives."

Scenes from the Workplace

BREAKING THE GLASS CEILING

Claire Werner never doubted that she would be a partner in her Wall Street securities firm. A graduate of a prestigious business school, but with a doctorate in economics, she taught for several years at a major university. She was the first woman hired as a market analyst in her well-regarded firm. Within two years she had become one of four senior portfolio managers reporting directly to a senior partner. Her clients give her the highest recommendations for her outstanding performance and over the past two years she has brought in the largest number of new accounts to the firm.

Despite the admiration of her colleagues and their seeming acceptance of her, there is a disturbing side to Claire's job. Most of her peers and some of the partners visit her office periodically during the day to discuss—in private—her opinions on market performance and financial projections. She is flattered by these private sessions and by the widespread respect for her opinions. Yet, despite these many private meetings, the CEO, Martin Greer, seems to downplay Claire's knowledge. At the weekly staff meeting, Martin invariably says something like, "Okay, let's get started and bring Claire up to date on some of the trouble spots." None of the others mentions that Claire knows as much as they do about what's going on in the firm. Claire is very disturbed but never protests this slight to her competence and knowledge, nor does she mention the almost daily private meetings where her advice is sought. As the only woman on the executive level, she prefers to be considered a team player and "one of the boys."

During the past year, one of her peers was promoted to partner, although Claire's performance clearly surpassed his as measured by the success of her accounts and the amount of new business she has brought to the firm. Now, having heard no mention of partnership for herself, she meets with her boss, one of the partners, and asks about the path to partnership. He replies, "You are doing great, Claire, but professors do not partners make. What happens if you are a partner and you make a huge mistake? How would you take it? And what about our clients? There's never been a female partner in the fifty-three years of our firm."

Claire knows she has grounds for taking legal action; she feels that there is clearly sexual discrimination at the firm regarding partnerships. If she decides to take legal action, through the federal Equal Employment Opportunity Commission (EEOC) or a private attorney, she thinks she can win. But she concludes that the emotional toll would be too much. Also, it would be extremely difficult for her to continue working at the firm while a lawsuit ensued, and she believes that the suit would affect her employability elsewhere as well. Too often, she hears women say, "File a lawsuit and it's career suicide." Whether this is true or not, Claire decides not to take any legal action, but she is devastated.

Without a rebuttal, Claire leaves the meeting with her boss and decides that she will leave the company to form her own investment firm, as many other women have done under similar circumstances.

What Should Claire Have Done?

Claire should have done the following:

1. Claire needed to make a strong case to the partners that her gender was a distinct value to the Wall Street firm. As a woman, she was able to attract women as clients. She understood their financial needs, their interests, and, often, their insecurities in investment strategy. She should have emphasized to her boss that being a woman is a tremendous asset in the changing customer base; over 50 percent of potential clients are now women. She should sell that point to the other partners as well and convince them of her worth to the firm.
2. Having experience in college teaching, Claire should have accentuated her skill as an educator. If the firm gives seminars on investment strategies, as most financial firms do, she should have volunteered to lead the seminars and demonstrate her ability as a speaker and facilitator of group discussion. If the firm did not yet offer this service, she could have offered to initiate seminars for men and women, including some seminars particularly for women.
3. The gender stereotypes should have been tackled directly. The stereotype that women "can't take it" must be negated. Claire, by her assertive behavior in meetings, by her self-documentation and announcements of progress, should have declared herself to be a strong woman and certainly not one who would "crumble under fire." Where was the boss's evidence that she would, in fact, do so?
4. Claire should have pointed out that she played a highly constructive role in meetings with staff and clients. She was a skillful negotiator and conciliator. She made people, men as well as women, feel comfortable in asking her questions in private. They trust her confidentiality and that she will not disclose others' weaknesses. She was a real team builder, and, most important, her performance was outstanding and she brought a great deal of business to the firm.

5. Claire did not know how to market herself within the firm. Her skills were tremendous in getting new accounts, understanding market performance, and using her background in economics for providing her with a sound intellectual base for her financial projections and sharing her expertise with others on the staff. Claire had to learn how to present herself—market herself—as a top economic and portfolio expert in the firm. She should have emphasized that being a woman was an asset, not a liability.
6. Claire needed to find a mentor. She should have identified one of the partners who seemed most supportive of her (and who met with her in private to seek her advice and opinions) and asked him to mentor her path to the partner track. She could have asked him for feedback on her personal style. Was she seen as too "professorial"—too academic and not practical in the real world? Or was being "professorial" seen as threatening to others with less academic backgrounds? She could have asked the mentor for feedback on her speech patterns, mannerisms, or social skills that may have been seen as not conforming to the Wall Street business norm.
7. Claire should have projected herself more at the staff meetings. For example, she should have stated firmly that she had knowledge of the subject at hand and in fact had offered counsel—in private—to a number of the staff on the same issue. She should have enlisted support—before the meetings—from her peers and senior staff, asking them to speak up about her abilities and advice. (Claire would have to be sensitive to the fact that some of her "advisees" might not want others to know that she had given them help in private, but she should at least have gotten them to acknowledge publicly her general skills and strengths.)
8. Claire should have documented her achievements—the number of clients she'd brought to the firm, especially the number of women, and the financial value of her portfolios. When she had her meeting with her boss to discuss the partnership, Claire should have had all her accomplishments—her assets, clients, and profit to the firm—clearly documented.

What Might Claire Have Said to Her Boss When Requesting Partnership?

Claire might have said the following: "Martin, we need to talk about my becoming a partner. I think you know the statistics of my career here.

I've prepared this folder, which I'll leave with you, documenting that I have brought in the largest number of new clients to the firm in the past two years. Being a woman has proven an asset: 60 percent of my new clients are women, and the dollar value of many of their accounts is among the largest in my portfolio.

"In addition, I have a plan to embark on a series of seminars for clients, both men and women, and perhaps separate seminars for women clients. Teaching is one of my strengths, particularly my ability to outline sophisticated strategies in a commonsense way. I've also boned up on the latest use of computer graphics for overhead presentations—actually, I do it directly from my laptop. I'd like your approval for marketing these seminars.

"As you may or may not know, my advice has been consistently requested privately by almost all our senior staff. My academic economics background and teaching skills have helped facilitate market analysis at the firm.

"Let's get together in a few weeks and discuss a timeline for partnerships. I would welcome feedback on additional skills you feel I need and any strategies we could use to get others on board to accept their first female partner. I believe that if you support me, others will clearly follow since everyone clearly acknowledges your long experience and expertise in the business."

A WORKER WHO IS DISABLED NEEDS TO TAKE SOME RISKS

Dan Turner is a wheelchair user and has been for most of his life. When he graduated from college with a major in computer science, he assumed that he was very marketable because of the growing demand for his skills. But he found it very difficult to get a job. Despite the Americans with Disabilities Act (ADA) and other laws against discrimination, Dan found that personnel people often were concerned about his ability to get to work and to maneuver around the workplace. Also, despite his excellent college record and background, there seemed to be doubts about whether he could perform successfully in a high-tech atmosphere. "I was defined by my wheelchair. Being African-American didn't help either."

Finally, through the help of an agency specializing in locating jobs for people with disabilities, Dan was hired by a large insurance company.

Dan was thrilled because he'd been hired for a job commensurate with his training. Actually, he was grateful to have any job at all after his grueling unsuccessful job search, which had lasted several months.

Once on the job, Dan carefully did the work presented to him by his supervisor, which involved preparing statistical reports on various claims filed. Dan decided, "I'm not going to take any risks. I'll be happy if I can just prove myself on this job. I like the atmosphere and would like to stay here as long as possible."

Dan was extremely pleased when he passed his probationary period. At his first formal appraisal meeting, Dan's supervisor, Mary Bratton, said, "Dan, we are pleased with your work. I look forward to your being with us for a long time in this position." Dan was, of course, glad that Mary was satisfied with his work, but he was also somewhat concerned because he got the feeling that Mary expected him to remain in the job indefinitely. He was grateful for the job but didn't want to view it as a total "dead-end" position.

Dan seemed well liked by his peers, and he'd developed a good relationship with several of his colleagues. Dan confided his concerns to Brad Graham, one of his colleagues in a related department. Brad said, "Dan, with your skills, you can certainly do more than your present job. Why don't you take more initiative on the job and develop some special projects on your own so that you can get noticed by some senior staff, as well as get Mary's attention?"

Dan was pleased that Brad thought he could go beyond the work he was doing, but he was scared. Dan was afraid that he might "mess up" or present a proposal that others think was foolish. He finally decided, "Maybe I should just be satisfied with things as they are. Why should I put myself at risk, when I have this 'safe' job?"

What Should Dan Have Done?

Dan should have done the following:

1. Dan should have seen himself as someone who could maximize his talents. Despite his difficulty in locating a job initially, he should have recognized that not all workplaces are the same. Perhaps his workplace was one of the increasing number that are willing to see beyond a disability to a person's actual talent. Even if his immediate supervisor saw his career as limited, others in the organization may have viewed his talents differently.
2. Once Dan felt comfortable on the job, he should have done some

research within the company to see how else his skills could be used and to determine if he had the knowledge to compete in some of the more advanced areas. He could have explored taking classes offered by his company or at the local university to make him more competitive. The world of computer technology changes daily. Not only would this have given him additional skills, but it would also have demonstrated to his boss Dan's ambition and determination to get ahead. (His boss might have felt that Dan was willing only to rely on his limited knowledge from his college program, without expanding further.)

3. Dan could have looked at the material his department was preparing to see if he had any suggestions for improving the reports prepared. He should have recognized that it may be hard for him to take risks. If so, he should have felt free to test out his ideas with his supervisor or other workers. Having a physical disability, as well as being African- American, may have contributed to his staying in the background. But he could have sought support for his ideas and his presentation of materials.
4. To get some additional visibility in the company, Dan could have affiliated with the diversity program in his company if there was one. For instance, there might have been a specific caucus or group for workers with disabilities. If so, he could have met others who have had special challenges to overcome and get support—moral and substantive—from them. Through such a group, Dan could have offered leadership to his organization on meeting the needs of workers with disabilities and techniques for reaching out to workers with disabilities who could contribute to the company. He could also have become involved with an African-American group within the organization, if any, getting advice from those who have been successful. Using his African-American background, he could also have helped the organization in recruiting talented African-Americans for job openings and possibly in developing market approaches.

What Might Dan Have Said to Brad?

Dan might have said the following: "Brad, you've been at the company longer than I have. Even though we're in different departments, can I run a few ideas past you? I think our department can use many more computer graphics in our reports. I have a creative side, but I don't want to go out on a limb when I present my ideas to Mary. She's pretty conservative. I may need some help from you with my presentation style, too. Believe it or not, I used to be on the debating team way back in high school. Maybe my persuasiveness in speaking would help me 'sell' my ideas to Mary."

What Might Dan Have Said to Mary, His Boss?

Dan might have said the following: "Mary, I am really glad that you are pleased with my work here. I want to let you know that I am enjoying this job tremendously. But further down the road, I'd like to be given the chance to demonstrate some of my special skills, especially in computer graphics. As you may not know, I am taking an advanced course at the local college. I'd like to show you one of the projects I am working on there that could be helpful in our departmental reports. I'd like to go as far as I can in the organization. Can I count on you to help me? "

Success Stories

MAXIMIZING YEARS OF EXPERIENCE AND EXPERTISE

Larry Rachman, a fifty-five-year-old white former businessman, has relocated to a city in the West and with his new Ph.D. has embarked on a new career as an urban planner in an inner-city community development organization. Hear him on the issue of age and how he overcame that barrier to become a success in his new field:

"I made enough money to retire, but I decided to continue being active and use my experience and skills to pursue a career that had long interested me. That's why I earned a Ph.D. in urban planning. I wanted to work for the public good, instead of just for profit. But was I a fool! I assumed that my business experience and impressive resumé, and a willingness to work for a minimum entry-level salary, would land me a job in no time. Wrong!

"Interview after interview landed me nothing. One of the interviewers even said to me, after seeing my resumé, 'I feel uncomfortable with you; you should be sitting where I am.' Even my intentions were questioned: Why would a man of my age, experience, and abilities want to start all over again?

"I realized I was seen as old and over the hill, not relevant to the current scene. So here's what I did: I made sure that all dates were deleted from my resumé. Second—and controversial, I know—I dyed my gray hair to a medium brown. Frankly, my new hair color alone took ten years off my appearance. In three weeks, I was offered two jobs and took the most promising one. If I ever doubted that appearance and image were essential, these offers sure proved me wrong.

"Still, I was a little self-conscious. My boss was twenty years younger than I was; my peers even more. I was seen as the 'Daddy'—clearly of a different generation. It took me three months to gain credibility. I acknowledged the knowledge and skills of those younger than I am. Clearly, I didn't come in like a 'know-it-all' authority figure. But I did use my core strengths, which were experience, good judgment, and a willingness to take risks in addition to the knowledge I had from my graduate program. Incidentally, my being white did not present itself as a problem for me or anyone else on the very diverse staff.

"My first success as a proposal writer, which was part of my job, was to find a funding organization that had never been tapped before. I presented myself to the funder, one of the major foundations in the area, and to the shock of my boss and peers, I asked for a very large sum. The amount was at least five times what the agency would ask from other funding sources.

"I could sense and assess the response to my proposal from the funder, with the realization that I had full confidence in the proposal's value. I could see the interest of the organization's representative and took the risk of asking for a large amount. And I got it!

"This was my first success in the organization, and within sixteen months I was appointed executive director. I didn't need to dye my hair anymore! I had proven my worth.

"Experience, knowledge, learned skills, risk taking, comfort with people. All these I had and maximized.

"I would not let myself define age as a deficit. I proved to myself and the organization that *my age was a positive*! "

"MY COMPETENCE, HUMOR, AND WARMTH OVERCAME THE STEREOTYPES"

And here's the voice of Ella Freeman, the first African-American regional executive of a national youth organization.

"I don't know if I had a plan to be at the top of the hill, but I always had confidence that I would do well in everything I tried to do. Maybe I felt that way because of my blackness and the odd pigmentation of my skin, a rare condition that gives me white pigmentation on parts of my face and hands. That pigmentation, combined with my very dark skin, always made me stand out. I always knew I was different. I know what it's like to be stared at and taunted.

"But I drew on the positives of being black. One positive was that I learned to overcome hostility and rejection. I assumed I was competent and that others who were hostile to me were just ignorant. I also learned that you have to take people where they are. I can face that and move on.

"Finally, after fifteen years in my organization, I was selected to be executive director. After that, two of the board members, very upper-class wealthy white women, wouldn't talk to me. But I ignored that and when I met them, I was very friendly. I smiled and said hello. I wouldn't let them get to me. It took awhile, but they came around. Maybe being black gives you commonsense. I knew that to succeed, I couldn't float. I had to work twice as hard as other people. I had strong management skills, but I also had people skills. A lot of blacks have this sixth sense of how to get along and who is behind you. I used that.

"I'm direct—a trait of many blacks from the East Coast especially. I say things 'like it is.' People know that I'm totally honest. When they ask for feedback, I'm going to say it straight. Maybe people are even a little afraid of me because of that. But I try not to be harsh or to deliberately insult others. I won't do that. I know what it's like to be on the receiving end.

"I also have a good sense of humor. So many white people seem stiff and formal to me. I think whites like my humor; it puts them at ease.

"I got ahead by being a decision maker and not being afraid to give forceful, straightforward messages. When I was first made a supervisor, I said to my staff: 'Take risks; you might mess up, but I'll protect you. Just don't hide it.' Yes, I took risks and encouraged my staff to do that, too. Sometimes we goofed and then fixed our mistakes, but by moving ahead we accomplished important things.

"I did the same with my supervisors. I would say, 'You hired me, now give me your support. You can give me suggestions, too, but I was hired to run the operation. So help me, but give me my head; let me really be in charge.'

"I am a mover and shaker. I flattered my bosses by giving them credit for supporting me, and shared credit with them for my victories. In turn they gave me more and more responsibility.

"I also told my staff how important they were, 'If you fail, I fail. But work hard—get out there or leave. Move. Do new things. Never stay still.'

"Even though I am warm and friendly, I knew that staff had to respect me. I would not let myself be buddies with any of them, white or black. I distanced myself from them socially.

"My advice to other blacks is: 'Help others see that blacks don't always fit the narrow mold that whites define for them. For example, my niece was in the highest academic group in her high school—all A's. But she was a cheerleader, wore bright clothes, hung around with some non-achievers. When honor roll time came, she was not given that award. Her mother had to go to school and protest. 'This girl had all A's—don't judge her by anything else.'

"What happened to my niece and the honor roll relates to me, too. I am in brighter clothes than most. I inject humor into my work environment. But my personality and clothes don't detract from my competence and my ability to achieve and make strides for the organization. I always accentuate my strong points, as well as those of everyone around me."

"MY BOSS LIKES DIFFERENCES; HE SAYS, 'YOU PUSH THE ENVELOPE'"

Michelle Cho, a Chinese-American, has had a successful experience building on her cultural background in her job as a television reporter.

"My 'positive' is my drive. Yes, many Asian-Americans have that, but what was different for me was that I chose a field that my parents didn't think was prestigious and respectable enough or safe and secure enough. They wanted me to be a doctor, a teacher, or at least a classical musician. But I wanted to be a television reporter. And I made it.

"I made it by killing myself. I accentuated that 'positive' of my culture. Hard work and excellence were always a part of the way I was brought up. When I was in grade school and I got B's, I was admonished that I could do better. When I finally did get A's, my parents didn't comment or praise me. It was just expected. In college, in addition to classes, I had two jobs, and then after graduation, two internships. I hustled.

"I also took risks. I knew that selecting a profession that my parents didn't respect was a risk. If I failed, it would be a deep humiliation for me in my family. But I knew that I had to take the chance. The hostility of my family about my career choice could have broken me down. But the more resistance I found, the thicker my skin became.

"Prejudice makes you stronger and helps you strive for excellence—even beyond the pressure of your own family. I spent the first five years of my life in Taiwan. I spoke three languages. When we moved to California permanently, I was one of only two Asians in an all-white neighborhood. Kids were cruel and harassed me because of my color and speech. Because of that I was determined that my English would be perfect. I would not be like my parents, who had accents. I knew that I was great at languages, and I was determined to perfect my English speech and writing. I used that skill to get ahead, to move from radio news reporting to TV reporting.

"I sometimes thought being Asian was a negative, but actually it was a positive. At first, I had self-esteem problems because I wondered, 'Did I get the job because I was Asian or despite the fact?' But I found a supportive mentor, a white woman, who said, 'You'll drive yourself nuts if you think only about your ethnicity. Tell yourself that everyone thinks they got a job because they're a woman or white or whatever. A lot of people don't give themselves credit for getting ahead. Forget about getting the job because of or despite being Asian. It doesn't matter. You're good. That's all that counts. Just be the best there is.' This advice helped me on my job at a radio station. After several months, I told the manager, 'You see, as an apprentice, I can do the work. I've proven myself.' Just saying that was a risk for me. I had to overcome my tradition of humility and non-assertiveness. But I made a decision not to just wait to be discovered, but to speak for myself and to get others to help me.

"On my current job, being Asian *is* a positive. My boss likes differences. He thinks that diversity brings creativity. He likes young people and diverse people. He says, 'It's because you push the envelope.' He likes my drive and energy and willingness to try new subjects and new emphases in my reporting. He's told me that he hired me because he thought that I wouldn't be stuck in traditional patterns and usual boundaries."

BEING GAY AND A LATINO WERE ASSETS

Juan Serrano is a director of special projects at a midsize university in the Midwest. "I consistently brought in huge grants to the university. None of my peers even came close to my record—the range and amount of grant money were far more than anyone else's. But I felt that being Latino and gay was holding back my career. I thought that several other administrators, with less of a track record, got more recognition. Although I didn't make an issue about being a Mexican-American or about my sexual orientation, I thought that most people knew I was both. If they didn't specifically know I was Mexican-American, I assumed they knew I was a Latino by my name and color.

"Since I am a practical man and had some good friends on campus, I thought that probably not everyone felt uncomfortable about my cultural background, and maybe not all the key administrators were homophobic. I decided to talk about my concerns about my place in the university with my immediate supervisor, the dean.

"Much to my surprise, the dean was happy to set up a meeting to discuss my career direction and my perceptions. What I anticipated might be an adversarial meeting turned out to be a very productive planning session. I soon realized that the dean really appreciated my work and fully recognized my contribution to the university. Moreover, I learned that the dean was a staunch supporter of mine in cabinet meetings, backing up my grant proposal topics.

"The dean and I agreed that, yes, there were some homophobic feelings among some of the cabinet members and other key university officials. However, they were in the minority and were rebuked publicly in meetings by the dean and others when they made any hateful or stereotypical comments.

"I agreed with the dean that, in addition to my success in getting grants, I am adept in building strong, interpersonal relationships with a wide variety of people. I explained to the dean that *personalismo* (interpersonal connectiveness) is a strong Latino value and perhaps I could use this cultural tendency more in my university work.

"The dean and I developed a plan for in-house workshops on diversity, including cultural differences and sexual orientation. Because I am an accomplished public speaker and relate well to people, the dean suggested that I be a leader in the workshop program. The dean told me that the university was committed to providing a workplace and an educational environment free of discrimination.

"I soon learned that I had a strong ally in the dean and I developed a specific action plan for educating the campus community. I realized that my Latino background and being gay were assets and would help me make an important contribution to educating the university about diversity. This was an important plus, in addition to my proven skill in getting grants and running academic projects."

Juan also discovered that "not everyone is hostile" and that sometimes it's a good idea to "call out the cavalry." Seeking support is a sign not of weakness but of strength and self-confidence.

Principles for Strategy 3, Accentuate the Positive

Much of the strategy for accentuating the positive can be summed up with the acronym RULE:

R Risk taking
U Uniqueness
L Learning
E Excellence

R Is for Risk Taking

Let's start with a key tactic for "making it": risk taking. This means that you are willing to make a decision or plan an innovative action—and take the risk that the action may fail. But the risk should be based on your research, your experience, your judgment, and your special knowledge of the situation. You have to be convinced that you have an idea or plan that will be successful and make a real difference to your organization. Then, don't be afraid to take the initiative.

But even though it's *your* idea, you can still talk it over with others before you present it to your boss. Talk to knowledgeable others before, during, and after you complete your plan.

And don't forget to make your boss look good when you complete a successful project.

One final note: In grade school, some of us remember, we learned a bromide—"elephants never forget." You may not have a clue as to what this saying means. But an African-American manager in the recording industry was stymied by a one-time bad experience. He was convinced that the bromide had another twist, "Managers never forget." This twist is something that you can probably understand easily. Obviously, he had one or more bad experiences with managers. We suggest yet another twist on the bromide. It is neither elephants nor managers that never forget—it is we.

We need to let go of past mistakes and errors. We should not let them deter us from taking new risks. Too often, though, instead of launching into a new assignment, we may hear a negative voice within ourselves constantly telling us, "Slow down, don't do this, don't do that. Remember the last time? Was that a disaster!"

Yes, often we, more than anyone else, hold ourselves back from success. Try to forgive yourself for the mistakes of the past—let them go! Learn from each task—both successful and unsuccessful. Then feel ready to take action, take risks—for success.

U Is for Uniqueness

"I have something special that men on my level don't," said an executive who is the only woman in the senior level of her organization. "Unlike most men, women are used to juggling their lives between work and home. On the job, my uniqueness is that I am not just singularly focused. I'm known for my ability to handle many tasks and to be adept at crisis management." A black manager said, "I'm liked for my expressiveness. That's a definite plus for me. So many white males have been brought up to hide their feelings. They find me refreshing and want to try out their ideas on me."

Both these people put a positive spin on their special characteristics. Both were realistic about their strengths and were able to build on them.

In a literal sense, the combination of *all* one's attributes makes each individual unique. No one attribute is unique if other individuals or groups share it. But a very important part of each individual's uniqueness is his or her cultural or group background, especially in a work setting where others may not share that background.

You have to internalize the reality that your cultural heritage or group characteristics have made you special for many reasons. One, you probably have overcome negative experiences, persevered, and shown the strength of your motivation to succeed. Others will usually notice your motivation and admire you for your perseverance. Two, you bring a bottom-line awareness of markets not readily known or understood by the dominant culture. And three, in several different ways, you're unlike everyone else. Some of you can "push the envelope," stretch, and, although comfortable with the dominant culture, you can add new resources, images, and perspectives in an increasingly diverse world. Your multi-language skills, your intense people skills, your discipline and ability to create harmonious relationships—all these are exceptional skills. These extras will help push you to the front if you can position them or reframe them to people of power and authority as distinct and positive attributes.

Once you appreciate the value of all your attributes, emphasize them and the benefits you can bring to the bottom line. Help others realize that your uniqueness is a special bonus that you bring to the organization.

L Is for Learning

In the 1990s one of the most popular management concepts was the "learning organization." The distinguishing characteristic of these creative and successful organizations is that they are constantly "learning"—new ways to do things, new ways to utilize staff, and how to use new technologies. Static organizations shrivel, and so do static individuals. No job—even the most menial—can stay the same and be successful. Learning new ideas and technologies keeps you "state of the art" in your field and in your work. Perhaps even more important, it keeps you, as an individual, alive and motivated. Doing the same thing—with the same tools—month after month, year after year, can be deadening to the mind and spirit. And, of course, to your career.

Being constantly open to new ideas, technology, and resources is another way for you to stand out from the crowd. Like the woman executive mentioned earlier, you can be the person whom people want to talk to when they want to know, "What's the latest in the field?" A key way to accomplish this feat is to be active in the professional organizations in your field, where you'll not only get information but make lots of contacts that can be helpful down the line.

Another imperative is not to stay in the same job but to seek other avenues for your old and new skills either within your current organization or in a different one. And in order to present your ideas effectively, perfect your speaking and writing skills. A successful African-American advises, "Be where the product is—not behind the scenes. Too many women and minorities stay behind the scenes. Do this long enough and that's where you'll end up."

If you want to get to the top of your organization, you have to learn the right track to get there. As mentioned earlier, it usually is important to seek a line position if you want to be in the top rung of your organization. What are the key jobs, assignments, people to know? Learn how your organization works by asking others, getting to know others. A Latino executive advised, "You have to constantly watch what's going on in an organization; observe and learn the organizational dynamics. The "politics of power" was a key watchword in my business school. Just learning that helped me get ahead."

Specific career strategies as well as organizational know-how are part of the learning process, as well as skills and information. And the key daily ingredient for tying everything together is *being organized*, from knowing what to do first at your desk in the morning to how to accomplish your long-term objectives.

E Is for Excellence

The underpinning of accentuating the positive is excellence. Without your maintenance of high standards of work and of producing more than what is needed or requested, all the other strategies will be empty and meaningless.

Throughout the book, you will read over and over that you have to work harder and be better than those who are members of the dominant culture. Many may assume that you are incompetent. This is especially true when you first start a job. Therefore, when you are an unknown and first arrive in your organization, look the best you can, do the best work you can, and make every effort to exude energy and enthusiasm.

Too often, your track record will not travel with you. You may have to start over with each new person you meet and let him or her know about your achievements or have others talk about them for you. How to do this is what you will learn in our next strategy, "Blow Your Horn."

SUMMARY

STRATEGY 3: ACCENTUATE THE POSITIVE

1. Constantly maximize your skills and your ability to implement your ideas.
2. Recognize your special background as a source of inner strength and as an asset to your organization.

STRATEGY 

BLOW YOUR HORN

Make Sure Your Organization Knows What You Can Do

"What does it take to be noticed here? I've worked hard. Kept my nose clean. My performance evaluations have been excellent over the past five years, and my bonuses reflect that. So why have so many others been promoted, given the choice assignments and all the other perks? It's like I am invisible, like I am not even here. I'm just a machine."

We've heard this refrain and similar stories from countless people of "difference" in organizations. The invariable refrain is "What does it take to get ahead here? Doesn't performance speak for itself?"

In their gut, these "others" still believe the Cinderella story—that someone will rescue them and make them stars or that performance speaks for itself and "if you build it, they will come."

Maybe yes, but most likely no. Unfortunately, performance is only part of the equation for success. Even if you are a paragon of accomplishments, you will not necessarily be discovered or recognized and appreciated and plucked from obscurity. Even if you build a baseball field, or a bridge or a department, don't believe that that's enough! Sure, you need the skills and accomplishments and the contacts we've talked about under previous strategies. But to get ahead, you have to be able to answer the question that's in everyone else's mind: "Who are *you*?" And just how do you do that? Well, you've got a horn. Blow it—sometimes in a muted way—*but blow your horn*!

What exactly do we mean by blowing your horn? Basically you have to let other people—as many as possible—know about your on-the-job accomplishments and about your other talents, skills, and experience.

People have to notice you—you have to be known by as many people as possible and be seen as indispensable, or at least very important, to your organization. Too often, workers' successes on the job are known only by their immediate managers (who often take credit for the work!).

You may think that blowing your horn means simply being able to tell people wherever you go about what you've accomplished. But be careful! Other people may see you as only promoting yourself, bragging, and implicitly putting others down. The knack of "blowing your horn" successfully is to let people know how you've helped the organization, without just flaunting yourself or showing off or bragging.

A famous professor of management said, "Be sure to blow your own horn because, if you don't, someone else could use it as a spittoon!" That's a pretty harsh admonishment, but the message is sound. Promoting yourself, marketing yourself, and selling yourself are as important to your success as your accomplishments and performance.

Those outsiders who have made it tell us that they did not simply leave their career up to other people. They did not sit and wait for others to recognize their value. They treated themselves like a product, with distinct features and benefits. They put together an advertising and promotion campaign designed to let senior executives know about their accomplishments and their value to the mission of the organization. In other words, *they learned how to blow their own horns*. They learned how to be visible—how to get people to notice them.

"Well, as the 'other,'" you say, "people sure do notice me." That's true, but not in the way you want. You want others to notice you for your strengths, your abilities, your vision, your value to the organization—not for your ethnicity, age, color, or gender alone. And that means an advertising campaign, subtle but powerful, that reaches the "right people" within your organization. Remember, a strong case can be made that, if a tree falls in the forest and no one is present to hear it, there is no sound. Make sure everything positive that you do makes a sound and that the right people are present to hear it.

In this strategy we will be looking at some techniques that successful people have used to their advantage. There are no guarantees. Not all strategies will work for you or progress at the same speed as they have for others. But we can promise you that if you do nothing, that's precisely what you will get in your career—nothing.

Unfortunately, cultural issues prevent some of us from creating our own advertising campaign to get people to notice us. So let's deal with these issues first.

Consider the following:

- *Blow your horn?* "Never," said a Latino middle manager. "In our culture we don't do that. If we speak up at meetings we feel we take the seat of honor away from our superiors. We don't like to show off. We believe things will come our way."
- *Blow your horn?* "Never," said a Japanese-American male, an executive in a social service organization. "We believe that the nail that sticks out is hammered down."
- *Blow your horn?* "Never," said a Ukrainian immigrant. "We've been afraid so long that we would rather be in the second row than the first."
- *Blow your horn?* "Never," said a male clerk with a disability. "We think others feel that we're lucky just to have a job at all."
- *Blow your horn?* "I try to, but it's so hard for a woman," said a vice president of a bank. "Our role is still to be the second sex—never to be seen as overly aggressive. If we ever do blow our horn, we must acknowledge our boss as instrumental in our accomplishments."
- *Blow your horn?* "Never," said a Vietnamese-American hospital technician. "You have to defer to others, listen and learn."

- *Blow your horn?* "We're not good at it," said an African-American investment banker. "Self-promotion is very hard for us. If we tout our success, whites think we're arrogant and blacks think we're 'big-headed.' Sometimes other blacks will even say, 'Who do you think you are? I knew you when . . .' "

Strategy 4, "Blow Your Horn," is surely one of the hardest for people not of the dominant culture to carry out. It is never easy to promote oneself, but for many people of difference, doing so seems almost impossible.

The cultural inhibitor is real and has to be dealt with. Many people who were not born in the United States, or who are strongly influenced by their cultural background, are not comfortable with this promotional strategy. An Asian-American woman said, "We feel we will be discovered by our work alone; our skills will be noticed." "Lightning will strike and we will be revealed," said a Korean-American salesperson.

A dilemma. But the first factor that must be identified and modified is the effect of cultural inheritance and how it has helped to block advancement. In the dominant American culture it is considered the norm to speak up at meetings and announce your ideas or the accomplishments of your department. Meetings have always been a great time to "show off," to reveal that you are a communicator, an innovator, a leader.

Now, a bit of caution here. In some of the higher echelons of white, Anglo-Saxon men, blatantly bragging about your accomplishments or position or people you know just isn't done. Modesty and "downplaying" are considered the more appropriate "interpersonal style." "When I hear people bragging about their jobs or money earned," said a CEO of a major manufacturing company, "I immediately feel they are really a 'nothing.' The real people don't have to talk like that. They don't have to because they—and others—know they're somebody."

One of the most important skills you need to learn is how to describe yourself in less than a minute. When someone asks you to "tell me about yourself," what are you going to say? How do you describe yourself without bragging or going into detail, and boring the other person to indifference about you? The answer is simple. Prepare and practice and make sure your presentation of self includes the following:

1. Your area of responsibility first (your title is secondary, and need not be mentioned unless it describes what you do).

2. A few words about your good fortune in meeting your goals or the initiatives for which you're in charge.
3. Your enthusiasm about the company and the support you have received.
4. A connection to the other person if possible.

Example: "I'm Gladys Cordiero, responsible for the company publications. The job's really been expanding, and I'm excited about covering the entire East Coast now. I've been so lucky to have a great staff who's interested in doing new things, and the company's really so supportive. Have you seen the new magazine article we just published on consumer satisfaction? I'd like your feedback on the article, and also let me know if there's anything we can do for your department."

The foregoing is an example of how to "blow your horn" without sounding like a person who brags too much about his or her importance. There are many other ways to do this. First, you have to be aware of the corporate culture. A senior human resources executive said that in her company, no one mentions one's title to others when introduced. "But it's perfectly appropriate to describe your function and the projects in which you're involved. Doing that doesn't seem like bragging."

An important strategy, then, is to watch others in the organization who are well known and respected. How do *they* act to promote themselves without aggressively flaunting themselves?

Another way is to have others "blow your horn" for you. Your boss, your peers, and your subordinates (if any) can praise you in front of others. A female project manager, responsible for quality control in a large food conglomerate, was complimented by a senior production manager for improving efficiency in one of the midwestern production sites. She thanked him and said, "I'd really appreciate it if you would tell my direct boss. That would help me a lot." That suggestion worked. The offsite manager called her boss several days later, and her boss, in turn, complimented her for the good work and for her productive relations with plant personnel. Her strategy surely worked better than "bragging" to her boss directly.

Remember the legendary Dizzy Gillespie, the great jazz trumpeter. He often used a mute in his trumpet to create beautiful melodic sounds, sounds so pleasant that millions of people listened to his music for hours on end. Prior to performing in public, at a jazz club, he worked on his sound in his studio. He practiced and refined his music before introducing it to the general public.

The lesson is quite simple—you should do the same. Practice your muffled horn-blowing techniques. Use a friend, someone in a support group, or the ever-faithful tape recorder (or personal computer for those who are more visual). Also, keep in mind that Gillespie was a superb soloist but performed even better within the confines of a combo. Your work group is your combo—stay in tune with them, and the harmonies will be much more appreciated by all.

Although you should consider muffling the sound often when you blow your own horn, do blow it—you may be surprised at the effect you have on others. Even the greatest trumpeters, however, also blow it hard, straight, and without a mute and still attract an appreciative audience. Knowing your audience is the key.

A big choice is yours. We're talking success now. Interviews with the most senior executives who are not of the dominant culture revealed that they had to push themselves. "We not only have to be better, and work 150 percent harder than white males," said an Asian-American senior insurance manager, "but we have to 'get real' and understand what's happening. We can't let our cultural inheritance of modesty and reserve block us. This is America."

Let's look now at some real-life case studies where the strategy of blowing one's horn was surely needed.

Scenes from the Workplace

"Tracked (or Is It Trapped?) in a Niche Market"

Ramona Padilla is stuck in the special markets niche of her organization. She has been extremely successful, at her job in a regional phone company, in expanding sales to the Latino community. Although a marketing specialist, she works very closely with the sales department and is given credit in the special markets department for increasing sales by more than 100 percent in the past two years. She is known as that "lively Hispanic marketing genius."

She is proud of her work and wants to be considered, in a reasonable period of time, for a senior executive role in her company. She is glad that the company thinks highly of her, but, wherever she goes, she is identified only as a specialist in the Latino community. People like her socially, but she feels boxed into being a one-note Latina. Unfortunately, for her, Ramona is great at marketing the phone company, but she isn't great at marketing herself. And ironically, she feels that people don't take her career seriously because she is so friendly and sociable.

Ramona is a second-generation Puerto Rican, living in New York. When people ask her where she comes from, she says, "The Island." Many people assume she means the island of Puerto Rico. She jokes, "I mean Long Island—that's where I grew up. And I went to college in upstate New York."

But even though she grew up on the U.S. mainland, she still holds on to characteristics of her culture. She had been socialized by her culture not to stand out, not to take credit away from others. And as a woman, she was told that it was not feminine to brag about yourself. She was told that when you play yourself up, it is always at the expense of others. She can promote a product, but she was brought up not to promote herself!

What Should Ramona Have Done to "Blow Her Horn"?

Ramona should have done the following:

1. Ramona should have understood the limitations of a socialization process that had inhibited her self-promotional abilities. In the dominant American culture, "advertisement of self" is an American norm. That's what this strategy is about. And as a woman, she had the added burden of finding the appropriate "style" that would be seen as neither officious nor overbearing but that nevertheless allowed her to be noticed and to shine.
2. She should have been active in city-wide Latino groups and be seen as an ambassador from her company ("Good place for Latinos to work"). Her company might have made her a senior executive, for public relations purposes, if she were a widely known figure in the community.
3. She should have been active in general marketing organizations such as the City Marketing Group, or Women in Marketing, or

in organizations specializing in her company's business, such as Marketers in Telecommunications.

4. Ramona should have become acquainted with the company's public relations people and attempted to get her accomplishments into the company newsletter. If she was a good writer, she could have offered to write articles for the newsletter. If she was a good speaker, she could have offered to be a member of the company's speakers' bureau.
5. She could have spoken to the director of marketing about her goals and possibly gotten to know, informally, the head of the department in which she eventually wanted to be a major player. She should have let these directors know of her interests, skills, and accomplishments and perhaps made some suggestions for new initiatives.

What Might Ramona Have Said to Her Boss?

Ramona might have said the following: "Scott, I know you think I've done a good job increasing the Latino market, but I also know that my skills can apply to other markets as well. If I could work with some of the other people who are targeting special markets, I could give them loads of ideas in effective market analysis, developing community contacts, brainstorming with on-staff personnel, maximizing focus groups for the broadest return, and many other strategies. I wonder—how do *you* see my strengths, and where else do you see me using them so I can advance in this company? I'd like to hear your ideas and then draw up a list, with you, of new areas where I can be of value."

THE INVISIBLE WOMAN

Leila Singh, a first-generation Indian-American woman, is an intelligent, hardworking financial analyst. Her academic credentials read like a *Who's Who* report. As a college intern for a large accounting firm, she has produced work that is very well respected. Both management and employees like her and work well with her. Upon graduation from graduate school, Leila is offered a permanent, full-time position as an analyst with the accounting firm.

During her first month of work, she gets to meet several senior-level executives and partners of the company. Most of them are in their sixties, white, and wealthy. They seem to be unaware of her position in the company, and a few assume that she is the new executive secretary. Leila thinks, "How am I going to break this point of view? What can I do to make them notice me?"

Six months pass, and her performance exceeds expectations. Her boss, Bob Nelson, although appreciative of her efforts and results, never seems to validate her accomplishments. She watches her boss and other male associates pal around, go out to lunch, and spend time together after work. She is certain that part of the reason she is never appointed to select internal committees is that she is relatively "invisible." In a staff meeting she hears the others talking about the new hardware system being installed and the new financial software program. In addition, she hears that the partners are all getting new state-of-the-art personal computers for their offices and laptops for their home offices. The irony is that these partners add new meaning to the terms "old school" and "computer phobic," while she is highly adept at computer technology.

She chuckles to herself as she remembers the same problem that the administrators at her temple had when they got their new systems. She recalls her endless teaching and hand holding as she trained them to use these new tools. What an experience! As she listens to her boss awkwardly explain the new computer system, she realizes that experience has nothing to do with her plight here. She is the "other." Skills she has aplenty, but she is young, a woman, and a dark-skinned Indian-American.

During the meeting, several people openly discuss the new software and some express dissatisfaction with having to learn the new system. Phil Alexander, the head of MIS, introduces the technical representative of the software company to explain and demonstrate the new system. As the demo is proceeding, Leila realizes that this is the same program she used in graduate school. "What a relief," she thinks. "I know this like the back of my hand. I'll just let my work speak for itself—then I'll get noticed for sure. This is the break I've been looking for. Now we'll see who gets the recognition."

Another six months pass, and Leila is still looking to be included in working committees or informal get-togethers. She wonders why no one has called on her to help with the new system—which is still not being used correctly.

What Should Leila Have Done?

Leila should have done the following:

1. Leila should not have expected to be recognized for her good work alone. Leila should have helped others recognize her skills and abilities—in other words, her value to the organization. Promoting oneself is a lesson that women in particular must learn well—because most have been socialized not to draw direct attention to themselves for fear of being labeled as pushy, arrogant, or "bitchy."
2. Leila should have accepted and internalized the simple truth that her actions did have a positive impact on her department and, yes, even company profitability in the final analysis. It is this connectedness to the "bottom line" that all minority employees must recognize and capitalize on if they are to blow their own horns effectively. One way to start would have been for Leila to keep a journal of any special achievements or accomplishments, no matter how small they may have seemed to her. This documentation would have proven useful to present to her supervisor when she requested a promotion but, just as important, it could have been a constant reminder of her own worth and self-esteem.
3. Leila should have spoken up at meetings when she realized that she had a particular talent that could be useful to the organization. Others might not have known about all of her skills and, if the truth about them is left unspoken, both she and the organization lose. Here is where blowing your horn becomes a business imperative. Failing to do so is like a vice president of finance keeping all the corporate money in an interest-bearing account—that's not maximizing the potential of the asset. The same is true for Leila. She didn't speak up, and her corporate asset (her talent) was not being invested wisely. Blowing her own horn was not improper, even by her own cultural standards; rather, it would have been a wise investment—for all concerned.
4. Leila needed to clearly demonstrate her expertise with the new software. Just as she volunteered to assist at her temple, she needed to do the same assertively at work. Unused knowledge is

wasted knowledge. Applied knowledge has power. She should have sought opportunities to help others. Remember, if you want inclusion, "you've got to have something to trade," as a wise manager told us.

5. Leila should have learned how to mount an advertising campaign for herself while still performing above expectations, similar to the campaign suggested for Ramona in the previous case study. Leila should have learned to blow her own horn—clearly and constantly and to the right people. She should have learned who the decision makers or power players were in her department and in the organization as a whole. Then, she should have made her pitch to them.

What Might Leila Have Said at the Meeting Described Above?

Leila might have said the following: "This is the same program I had to use in one of my college courses. I am very familiar with it, and I know how we can use it here. I would like to offer my services to anyone here to explore how the company could maximize the use of this software. In addition, I can act as an intermediary between the software vendor and the organization to establish an in-house training program. This coordination should shorten the learning curve, save training costs, and make more of us more effective, faster."

Leila could also have scheduled some time at the next meeting and said: "During the past few months I have had the pleasure of helping nine associates learn the new software. At this point, they have the ability to analyze, cross-reference, and construct an array of 'what-if' questions. These inquiries have allowed them to decrease their response time to our clients by 10 percent and allowed them to provide several different options based on the simulations they created using the new program. I would like the opportunity to expand this effort during the next few months—with your endorsement, of course. Feel free to tell others of my consultation efforts and my interest in helping others on the new software."

Still need convincing? Let's hear, then, the voices of successful "others" who have blown their horns effectively, subtly, and to their advantage.

Success Stories

OVERCOMING A CULTURAL RESISTANCE TO SELF-PROMOTION

Tom Hiromura, a Japanese-American, is a city official who also knows the benefit of blowing one's horn. He said, "I emphasize organizational goals and needs and my ability to meet those needs. Most Japanese-Americans are not socialized to promote themselves. They wait for their abilities to be noticed and rewarded, but in America it doesn't work that way. In addition, we're taught that if you tell someone that *you're* great, it means *they are not.*

"But there's a way of getting around that. And this is what I did. When I worked with an all-white staff in the mayor's office of a major city, I became recognized by demonstrating my writing skills. I wrote memos about the mayor's speeches, complimenting him but offering suggestions on other ways of expressing his ideas for a diverse audience. But I knew that memos don't usually get to such a high person. So I cultivated a friendship with the deputy mayor because I knew that the deputy would send the memos up to the mayor. Thus, in effect, the deputy was blowing my horn. And it worked. I became the senior advisor to the mayor, and my political fortunes started there.

"Communication skills are the pathway to success. I learned that writing is important, but public speaking is a must if you want more power. To be seen as a leader, you must have that skill. A lot of Asian-Americans avoid that—it's too uncomfortable. But you must take a risk, and I did. I joined Toastmasters and practiced speaking with that group. I even entered a local speaking competition and came in second place. This gave me confidence in my abilities, and I asked to be on the program for a statewide conference. People now see me as leadership material. I'm on my way up."

• — •

"POWER TALK" FOR CREDIBILITY

Dorothy Lowe is an assistant director of public relations in a large telecommunications firm. "As a woman in a wheelchair, I am very aware of the stereotypes most people have of the disabled," she said. "I know people are gaping at me, but I do not allow myself to be lowered or denigrated. I don't kid myself; I allow myself to see myself as others see me. But I also try to judge my audience—one by one. I take a three-step approach: (1) I hone and then use my skills as leverage in order to be seen as a professional, (2) I emphasize what I have in common with others, and (3) I promote myself and my successes.

"Number one is obvious. I work 100 percent harder than anyone else. Number two—making others comfortable—precedes my promotion of myself. I use immediate eye contact with everyone I meet. I subtly bring into conversation my successful marriage, my daughter, and my travels.

"Then I go for number three, the power talk. I talk about my ability to deliver results. I talk about creating, implementing, and delivering. My projects create revenue—that's the bottom line. I promote myself by talking first about how my programs affect marketing concepts and what I've accomplished. I always talk results first, then *how* I did it.

"I blow my horn not only for me, but for all disabled people. I am committed to the goal of being a role model for others. Do you know I even get on the dance floor, in my wheelchair, with my husband to change people's perceptions of what a person with a disability can do? I will not have an attitude of humiliation and embarrassment. On the contrary, I think of myself as in the positive normalcy mainstream. And I never stop telling people what *I can do for them*."

• —— •

VISIBILITY IS THE KEY

"I know I'm a 'two-fer,' " said Selena Johnson. "Yes, I'm the highest ranking woman *and* a black at a national financial institution. And how did I do it? Skills are one thing; I have them, but *visibility* is the key. Believe me, if you're black you get noticed whether you like it or not. What's important is getting visibility by doing something important for other people in the organization.

"I am active inside and outside my organization. I'm an important figure in the National Association of Negro Business Women and, through that, I not only sharpened my organizational meeting skills, but I've brought in business for my company. And I let the company know it. 'I can sell so-and-so this,' I say to my bosses; 'I know this person who is on the board of a large communications organization.' My contacts are enormous. I meet black women who are leaders in their companies, and I leverage those relationships. It is essential to join professional groups not only for your own emotional support but also for the power you get from knowing others.

"And, internally, I'm just as visible by supporting all the top executives' favorite charities. I go to everything that I'm invited to. You can't believe how many rubber chicken dinners I go to in a year. Boring, yes, but everyone knows me and owes me.

"I promote myself by giving credit to my bosses in all my projects. If you give only yourself credit for your success, it looks like you're self-serving, and not a team player. When I initiate a project I get my superior's approval and then, when it's successful, I say it's *our* idea.

"My advice to young people coming up is to gain visibility by emphasizing the accomplishments of your work team. Because I'm so well known, I know that my name will always be mentioned when a top job comes up related to my skills. I'm there—a major player—and can't be ignored or overlooked!"

GETTING CLIENTS TO BLOW YOUR HORN

Raul Pacheco is the only Latino in his midsize insurance firm. He has risen to a senior position despite many obstacles. Describing his experience, he says, "As the only Latino in my company, I was patronized by most of the staff when I first got here. I was given the worst accounts where the growth potential was small. But I was told, 'Oh, I'm sure you can make something out of this. We have confidence in you.' I could hear the snickers of the other salesmen as they smiled (or was it smirked) to each other.

"But I showed them up. I did make something out of those territories. My skill is getting clients to like me. I built trust in the community by building personal relationships. My clients knew I would come through for them. I would explain the policies clearly and honestly. I wouldn't be condescending like the way I had been treated. What happened was that my clients spread the word like wildfire. One insurance policy led to another. Although many of the original clients were relatively low-income people, some of them had wealthier relatives and acquaintances. One of my original clients even referred me to his employer, and I ended up selling him a major policy. As I made inroads in more upscale neighborhoods, my reputation continued to grow. My satisfied clients were my best promoters."

Raul didn't have to "blow his horn" for himself. He had a host of customers who did it for him! And as his client base grew, his organization noticed him.

The strategy, then, that these four "others" used to be successful was to get the organization to *notice* them. They all did just that by "blowing their horn,"—not blatantly, but subtly without others' realizing that a campaign for visibility was going on. Your organization's senior leadership—your boss and higher—must notice you if you are to be successful. Sort of obvious, right, but how can they notice you?

Let's begin by introducing you to another acronym for your use: NOTICE. First we will give you a brief rundown of the words that make up the acronym and then we will explore each word in depth.

N	Network, network, network. Get to know as many people as possible and let them know your abilities. Also review Strategy 2, "Call Out the Cavalry."
O	Organization first. Get involved in the big picture of the organization, not just the minutiae of your job. Know the organization's bottom line and how it's measured.
T	Timeliness. Know when and in what framework you can blow your horn. Watch how it's done in your organization.
I	Inspire others by your energy, enthusiasm, and appearance.
C	Challenge yourself. Take risks, stretch your creativity, prove stereotypes wrong.
E	Educate others, share your expertise. Be a resource both in and out of the organization.

N-O-T-I-C-E

N IS FOR NETWORKING (TO ACHIEVE VISIBILITY)

In Strategy 2, "Call Out the Cavalry," we talked about the importance of having relationships with as many people as you can. Yes, networking is an essential key to success because you make contacts with others who can help your career. But another aspect to networking is often overlooked. To some people, "networking" means giving people your business card and then waiting for something to happen. This is a tremendous mistake. Successful networking means building relationships that are of mutual benefit. This takes time. Only after you have built a relationship can networking pay off.

The payoff is that once you have the relationship, those people can learn about your strengths and competencies. With people who like you, it is comfortable to "blow your horn." People aren't going to help you *only* because they know you and like you. They have to also think you have something to offer *them* and others they contact in your behalf.

Networking offers you a chance to meet people whom you might not ordinarily encounter or have access to. This is a way of getting visibility, promoting yourself, and getting the power players in the dominant culture to notice you.

Demonstrating that you can be comfortable with all kinds of people and that they can be comfortable with you is a way of promoting yourself. An African-American faculty department head was invited to the college President's Ball. She knew that she would be the token black, and one part of her said, "Don't go; don't sell out." But she knew that at this party she would meet very important people in her academic world. "I overcame my cynicism," she said. "I performed for the occasion. And you know, it wasn't awful. I met a dean of faculty from another university to whom I related my latest research on educational theory. He was very much interested in my research and invited me to present my findings at a regional conference he was chairing. I learned that you can't underestimate the mutual comfort factor—it is an extremely important skill in organizational life. And I learned too that it's easier to be a prophet in places other than your own town. The dean I just met seemed even more impressed with my research than people at my own college."

O IS FOR ORGANIZATION

"O for organization" means putting the organization first. It means selling your skills in terms of what you can do for the organization. A highly successful Asian-American male said, "Every day you have to think,

'How does my daily activity promote the vision and mission of the organization?' I do my job but try not to sweat the small stuff and get caught in the minutiae of my work. I read everything I can about every aspect of the business. I send memos to my peers on ways we can collaborate on joint projects." An African-American middle manager agreed. "I'm seen as a team player. I volunteer for as many company functions as possible. I chair the United Way Committee, and when the company needed a representative to a community dinner, I volunteered. You can't forget me. I'm here—*and how* I am!"

A female bank manager also agreed. "I flaunt myself, but appropriately. I keep a portfolio with all my accomplishments and awards—within the bank and in the community. The portfolio bowled people over when I applied for a promotion."

A Puerto Rican executive also used this strategy. "I'm here because there's nothing like hard work. Not only did I excel in my own area of expertise, but I volunteered for work that no one else wanted. In organizations within and outside the company, I volunteered for the job of recording secretary. Because of those volunteer jobs, I was seen as essential and an important contributor to the organization. My name was on all the minutes, so everyone knew who I was. Best of all, I needed to contact important people to verify my minutes or to gain additional information. I made contacts with major company players that way."

Another sure way to get noticed is to talk the "organization language." Usually this means being known as someone who has a "bottom line" perspective, who is interested in "measurable goals." A female programmer's boss was an unpopular but powerful executive. He was a stickler for laboriously detailed reports. The programmer said, "I got his attention because I did things his way. He wanted details; I provided them. Others of his employees balked at this style. Not me. I mimicked my boss, and got my reward. I was promoted!"

Select role models and be aware of how these organization "winners" prepare their written reports and presentations for meetings within the organization and for outside clients; use the company's preferred language and formats. Sophisticated and easy-to-read charts, overheads, and graphics—all these can get you noticed as contributing to the organization. Remember the Dizzy Gillespie metaphor of being in harmony with the organization and staying "in tune."

T IS FOR TIMELINESS

Blowing your horn can be tricky, as mentioned earlier. It can be a turnoff to many white males and females as well as to some members of other cultural groups, many of whom were raised to be understated and suspicious of blatant bragging or flaunting. Therefore subtlety and timeliness are important. Don't brag about something in an abstract way by saying, "I can improve sales" or "I know all the key players." But when you have finished a specific task, a project, or an important report, send it on to the boss with a note summarizing the results and stating how glad you are that it worked out so well. If you head a department, give your staff credit too. Extolling your department is a subtle way of touting yourself.

A Filipina-American, a middle manager in a software company, said, "I push myself to talk about myself and my accomplishments. It's not easy for me. I was not brought up to do that. So until the results of my work are indisputable, I'm modest; I almost go undercover. But when my work is really on the winning track, I let people know. I celebrate our unit's accomplishments by having an office party and inviting key staff from other departments to come also. So I'm not only making others aware of my achievement but also showing my skill in building staff morale by blowing the horns of others who have helped me."

A female senior director of a major nonprofit organization said she keeps a record of all her initiatives and their outcomes. "At the end of the year, I do a report on my activities and send it on to the president of the organization, for his information." Another woman, an immigrant from India, said, "Before my yearly performance review I submit information on every project that I have worked on in the past year. Everything is fully documented with bottom-line results noted."

A Latino manager overcomes his reluctance to brag or "blow his horn" by emulating the norms of the organization. "At monthly meetings with the CEO, almost all the managers take that opportunity to laud themselves and their departments' achievements. I play the game now and do that too. That's the time to be heard, and I make sure that I'm on the playing field.

"What I have learned, too," he said, "is that, although it's hard for me to be the first one to talk about myself, it's sure better than being last. Everyone's attention is gone by then or else they think you have to say something just to look equal to the others."

"I used to wait until someone was finished talking before I would say something," said a Chinese-American executive. "I learned you have to speak out, push yourself; otherwise you are ignored. The stereotype of the quiet, submissive Asian works against us even when we do speak up. People think, 'It can't be that important because it's only an Asian person saying that.' So I learned I had to be outspoken to make my accomplishments known and get credit for my work."

"I feel it's important to tell others about significant results soon after the project is completed," said an African-American manager. "Otherwise it seems like old news. On the other hand, you have to remember that you don't show how successful or important you are when it is someone else's moment to shine. You don't want a reputation for 'raining on someone's parade' or 'stealing their thunder.' You have to plan your time to shine so that it doesn't distract or take away from someone else."

Yes, timing is important when it comes to blowing your horn. Three vital points: (1) Don't rain on someone's parade when that person is publicizing his or her achievements, (2) in a group situation, when it's the *norm* for everyone to brag, don't be last—you look like an afterthought, and (3) remember the axiom: When opportunity knocks, open the door.

An example: If, in the elevator, you meet a high-level executive who you thought didn't even know of your existence and he or she surprises you by casually asking, "How's it going?" you can just say, "Fine," as most people probably would. But there's another way to go. In half a minute you could tell him or her how fantastic your project is doing and suggest a meeting along with your manager to discuss the project's implications for the company's goals.

Will this work? Maybe yes, and maybe no. But there are no down sides to this strategy. You don't look like a shy wallflower, and your enthusiasm is seen as a true commitment to the company's goals. And, most important, everyone likes good news—and you're the bearer of that.

I IS FOR INSPIRE

"I" is the fourth letter of NOTICE—our acronym for this strategy. Attitude is contagious. Your enthusiasm, energy, and drive will inspire others—and will be mirrored by others. You have to identify the areas of your job and the people that really excite you. (If there are none, you might want to seek another job!) Your positive attitude makes people want to be around you and makes them feel good. A Latino male, a bank manager, said, "You must love what you do and show that. It inspires others. Also it inspires your staff when you acknowledge their work. It makes them feel that what they do is important. You've noticed them and have told them so."

An executive who uses a wheelchair supervises a staff of three advertising managers. His physical disability is severe, yet he is always cheerful, manages to go everywhere, and is enthusiastic about all of life, as well as about the organization. He inspires his staff with his unbridled enthusiasm. "My staff blows my horn," he says. "They're the ones who tell others of my accomplishments. I'm lucky that, despite my disability, I have a brain and strong skills. And my zest for life and for my work shows. And, in turn, my staff tells everyone else about me."

C IS FOR CHALLENGE

Proving yourself and networking for maximum visibility require planning, risk taking, and challenging yourself. How can you spend your time in a top-priority way that also gains you visibility and notice? Planning takes time. One woman, the highest-ranking female of her financial management firm, said, "You have to spend your time in the areas which show off your abilities. My best skill is my speaking ability. So I use that to the hilt. I accept any request to speak at meetings and always volunteer to make departmental presentations. I'm also almost six feet tall, and I deliberately wear heels to look even taller."

Challenging yourself means risk taking, but the payoff is great. An Asian-American man, a competent manager, tended to be reticent about speaking. However, he observed that all the people who had "made it" were excellent speakers. Public speaking was not his thing. On the other hand, he knew he had to stretch if he was going to be noticed, appreciated, and promoted. He accepted the challenge. He began by joining an Asian-American community organization. He gave a generous contribution to the organization and was placed on the board. He spoke at meetings and, in time, got better and better. "It wasn't easy for me," he said, "but I felt this was a low-risk situation and I could do my practicing there."

A year later he was asked to be a vice president of the community organization. He rose to that challenge and used it to get ahead. He invited his superiors at work to a community conference he chaired. Not all the senior executives whom he invited came. But the ones who did were amazed; they had no idea he had strong leadership qualities and was a confident speaker. And for those who did not come, the invitation was an impressive, subtle way for him to blow his horn.

Challenge yourself—understand how you can stretch your productivity and creativity to improve the organization. A young woman who was known only as a good technical researcher by her employer realized that her department was unsuccessfully interconnected with the production department. She told her boss that she wanted to conduct a meeting with her counterparts in the production department, particularly because of her organization's recent merger with another large company. She said she was willing to organize and run the meeting. Her boss was surprised that she would take this initiative and encouraged her. As a result, she was seen in a totally new way. Her boss saw her as an initiator, having the organizational goals in sight and having the leadership skills to conduct the meeting. Her boss and the members of the other department all saw new facets of her skills.

One of the most difficult challenges of all when you are the outsider is to overcome the stereotypes that people have of you because of your gender, race, ethnicity, or age. An Indian-American woman knew the stereotyping she faced. "It is assumed that we can't speak well or have difficulty with writing skills," she said. "Even though I have a Ph.D., people always seem amazed at the quality of my reports. When I interview for jobs, I always bring a sample of my writing to dispel the stereotype. The challenge to me is that I have to overcome my cultural tendency to be humble. I have to let people know about my accomplishments. Maybe that's bragging, but I have to bear the discomfort."

A young Korean-American woman was told by an assigned mentor, "Look, because you're young and a woman, people will not take you that seriously. So speak up at meetings in a louder voice than is normal for you and assertively shake people's hands." "I thanked him for his help," she reported, "but knew this was not going to be easy for me. My voice is low, and I am modest and not as forceful as I should be. But I took the challenge and made a conscious effort to talk in a clear, loud voice, look everyone straight in the eye, and shake hands firmly. I'm doing well in my job, got a promotion after only two years, and maybe adopting my deliberate, assertive stance was the challenge I needed. I'm sure not the same at work as I am at home, but I know I have to adopt the cultural norm of my organization if I'm going to make it there."

E IS FOR EDUCATING OTHERS

E is the last letter of our acronym, NOTICE. An essential way of demonstrating your value is to educate others, to share your expertise with them. You have to show others that you can help them do their jobs better—make *them* look better. The word is then spread that you are an important resource to others. You not only do your job, but you help others do theirs. Your skills are shown to be broad and transferable to other tasks. Knowledge is power, but shared knowledge creates value for you in a larger sphere than your narrow unit.

Of course, you have to start somewhere. A woman who was a director of training for a large national nonprofit organization had good writing skills. Informally, one of the other directors told her that he hated report writing. "No problem," said the woman, "I love writing; let's have lunch tomorrow, and I'll be glad to look your report over." So he came to her for consultation about his writing and was the first of many who made the trip to her floor to ask for help. The word had spread—rapidly, as it does in most organizations. If you educate others you will be seen not only as very helpful within your own span of control but also as an important resource for a range of activities and skills. And, even more important, you will be seen as one who facilitates the growth and development of others. The training director's reward was a promotion within three years to head all of human resources and organization development.

An African-American marketing analyst agreed that educating others, sharing your skills, was a "ticket" to getting known. "I saw that people in my department were having trouble with some statistical analysis. It was one of my areas of expertise, so I helped whomever I could. Several people were really surprised when they learned I knew this thing cold and that I was willing to help them do it, too. Pretty soon, other employees began to spread the word about me."

Note that, in the voices of successful "others," many of the strategies of NOTICE were used with great success. Dorothy Lowe, the disabled woman, used her energy and resolve to inspire others around her.

She caused people to think of her in terms of her programs and results rather than her "difference."

Selena Johnson used networking to get ahead, both in and out of the organization. By making valuable contacts, she also showed her value to the organization's bottom line.

Raul Pacheco accepted the challenge of overcoming the organization's view of him—that he would be unable to succeed because he was a Latino. He used his skill in forming relationships and networked for success.

Tom Hiromura, the city official, used the strategy of educating others and addressed the needs of the organization as a whole.

All four were successful because they took risks, stretched their creativity, and proved stereotypes wrong.

So remember the acronym NOTICE when you ponder Strategy 4, "Blow Your Horn." Don't say, "I can't, I can't." Wrong. You *can* learn how to get higher-ups to notice you by networking so that others know of your skills, by keeping the larger interest of the organization always in front of you, and by remembering timeliness when you "blow your horn." That includes never putting others down while promoting yourself but, instead, acknowledging the accomplishments of others when you tout yourself. You can inspire others with your drive, energy, and enthusiasm—and even your appearance. (Review Strategy 3, "Accentuate the Positive.") You can take risks and stretch yourself by accepting challenges to get ahead, and by educating others who will blow your horn for you.

SUMMARY

STRATEGY 4: BLOW YOUR HORN

1. Recognize how cultural messages are barriers to blowing your horn.
2. Learn the difference between blowing your horn and showing off or being a braggart.
3. Blow your horn about your on-the-job accomplishments. Document everything.

4. Blow your horn about other skills, talents, and experiences that have not yet been demonstrated on the job. Share those skills.
5. The purpose of blowing your horn is to have others notice you. Use the acronym NOTICE, detailed in this strategy, to become visible.

STRATEGY 

BUY IN, DON'T SELL OUT

Adapt Your Cultural Style to the Organization's

"I think organizations want it both ways," said an African-American manager. "They hire people specifically for their diversity yet expect them to behave in a homogeneous fashion on the job." The expression of this seeming paradox appears to be the mantra of too many women and ethnic minorities whom we have interviewed over the years. On the one hand, organizations have a culture that has brought them a degree of success. On the other hand, the new hires bring cultures that are equally valid and can potentially add to that success, yet their culture may be vastly different from that of the hiring organization. Can women, ethnic minorities, gays and lesbians, and people for whom English is not the first language work successfully inside an organization and still maintain their individual identity? Or must they don the attire of the traditional male "forty-two long" suit, with the attending behaviors, to be accepted—let alone to succeed? Listen to the voices of many people in the workplace today who are not of the dominant culture as they deal with this adaptation issue.

- "To succeed, you have to give up a part of your culture," said an African-American woman. "Blacks tend to talk too much—we like to massage words. That's got to stop."
- "To succeed," said an older worker, "you have to keep up with the local rock star, or rock music. You have to show that you're with it, even if you hate that music."
- "To succeed, you have to modify your appearance," said a Latina woman. "I adapted by dressing less flamboyantly and giving up my emotional style."
- "To succeed, you have to play against every stereotype about you," said a Pakistani-American man. "Even if you're second generation, there is an assumption that you can't speak or write properly. I am constantly proving others wrong. I speak perfect English and take every opportunity to show that."
- "To succeed, you have to change your style of thinking," said a Latino male. "A lot of Latinos are impatient with details. Our minds take a leap; we are intuitive. We have to take a systematic approach—not leaps."
- "To succeed, you can't always stay with your group," said an Asian-American woman. "So many of our group are uncomfortable socializing; we must overcome that and mix socially with others."
- "To succeed, you have to read into what whites say, and figure out what they want to hear in response," said another African-American male.

Sound like selling out? Are those who buy into the dominant culture of the organization traitors to their own group? Have they forsaken their heritage? If so, is this justifiable? Are such people hypocrites, persons without self-respect? Do these statements of members of diverse groups mean that to succeed you cannot be yourself? Can we divide our personal and professional identities? And if we do, can we live with ourselves?

Sadly, too many people think that any subordination of one's heritage constitutes "selling out." Let's take a closer look at the differences between " buying in" and "selling out," because achieving success depends on your knowing the difference.

Let us say from the onset that this is an intensely personal decision. What one person perceives as "selling out," another person sees as accommodating behavior. Who is the final arbiter of "right"? We suggest the following guidelines for consideration in employing this essential strategy of "buying in" and not "selling out."

1. Your fundamental value system, that which you hold close to your heart, is the final arbiter of "right." If your values—which you learned as a child, tested as an adolescent, and solidified as an adult—are in direct violation of or contradiction with the organization's values, and you discard your values, you could be in danger of "selling out."
2. If you know yourself—have validated your talents, skills, and abilities—and perform a function or accept a position well beneath your talents, you could be in danger of "selling out."
3. If you accept, without question, the culture of an organization that flaunts its discrimination against or disrespect for your culture, you could be in danger of "selling out."

One way to look at this issue of "buying in" is to realize that we play many roles in our lives and in each role act somewhat differently based, in part, on the expectations of others. We assume different personas in different situations and to meet different expectations. In other words, we do not act or speak the same way when we are with our parents, our children, our spouses, our friends, or our bosses. Our social intelligence tells us that we cannot react the same way to different people. And we don't.

We don't have psychological problems with our change of persona with different people. We easily live with the fact that all personal interactions involve some form of adaptation. We all act differently in different situations—even within our own culture or our own "world." We might act more respectfully to an older member of the family than to a peer; we all would act differently to a boss than to a co-worker, a best friend, or our own children. We all act differently to people with different personalities and interests. Some people are "tough," others very "sensitive," some "shy"; some appear "all knowing." The rhythm of our speech, the speed of our discourse—these vary with what we think most fitting for our conversation with another person. With our sports friends, we may be "macho" and talk in terms of scores and best footwork. With our more intellectual friends, we talk of ideas, books, or films; our vocabulary is wider, our phraseology more sophisticated, our demeanor more serious.

Effective people—whether managers or co-workers—always adapt their behavior to differences in people, whether that difference results from status, personality, or interests. Adapting to an organization's culture is another form of adapting to the social expectations of the world in which we operate.

Yes, we change and adapt our communication style, our patterns of dress, and our selection of conversational topics according to the person we are with, the function we are attending, the part of the country we live in—to mention just a few criteria.

Thus, we are adapting our communication style all the time, and we never think we are two-faced, or are giving up our own ethnicity, gender, or culture as we define it. We're just responsive people, who understand the normal way of self-presentation in different situations.

But besides dress and communication style, other, perhaps more basic, work accommodations—such as timeliness, balancing work and family issues, and work norms of assertiveness versus compliance— may come into question. If you consciously make accommodations to the corporate culture on these issues, without turning your back on your basic values and without disrespecting your culture, you could be making strategic decisions to succeed. For many people, this is a thin line of distinction. You must decide for yourself what is right for you. However, be ready to suffer the slings and arrows from others in your group who may perceive your actions as "selling out." To paraphrase Abraham Lincoln, you can't please all of the people all of the time. But you must please yourself.

Take, for example, the famous jazz musician "Fats" Waller. In the Broadway play about his music, "Ain't Misbehavin'," the lyrics to one of the songs could be a prescription for making it in corporate life. To paraphrase, he tells us to "Find out what they want and how they want it, and give it to them just that way." In other words, identify the corporate culture, observe those who are successful, and follow their example.

But—and this is a big but—be certain that your behavior is not a violation of your basic principles and values.

Corporations and professions have different cultures as powerful and intense as those of any ethnic group. We find that when we move from one corporation to another, we have to begin all over again to learn its cultural style, values, communication patterns, and work norms. Let's look now at some of the ways corporate cultures differ from each other:

- Hierarchy: formal or informal
- Timeliness: punctuality or flexibility
- Dress codes: Strict or flexible
- Political views: conservative, liberal, or not significantly important
- Communication style: authoritative or collegial
- Staff relationships: functional or personal
- Speech: formal or colloquial; louder or softer

These are some of the areas in which accommodation is the key to "making it." But again, you must be comfortable with the notion that you can modify your behavior and still be true to yourself and your group. An African-American male said, "I define the issue differently; I'm certainly not a 'sell-out.' The organization is the culture I'm part of. I'm 'buying in,' and I can adapt. What many whites don't understand is that most blacks are 'bi-cultural'—they grow up learning how to act in both the white world and the black world." A Dominican-American male said, "Whatever challenges I faced, I never forgot where I came from. I gained strength from my background and sense of identity. I realized that my task was to integrate my new experiences with the values of the past. I never saw it as a direct conflict, but a challenge to find the right way to be accepted and to accept myself." These voices tell us that, yes, you have to adapt in some way to fit the organization's norms, but doing so does not mean you have to give up your identity.

Everyone knows people who completely assimilate and try to act totally in the style of the dominant culture. Yet, because of their skin color or their sexual orientation, they are still not accepted by a discriminatory organization. Sadly, in some organizations nothing will work, and you may have to confront the fact that despite all your adaptive measures, it is not appropriate to work in an organization that is clearly antagonistic to you. For example, some organizations are highly homophobic, and it is unlikely that a known gay person could make it to any position of leadership in them.

At face value, you may not fit into your organization. It is too different from your style and values. For example, as a Latino you may be used to flexible attitudes about time unless there is a definite reason for punctuality and the organization has strict time demands. You are used to being friendly and interacting socially with co-workers, and the organization is uptight and formal. As an African-American, you speak in a expressive way, and your clothes are highly individualistic and ahead of style while your organization has a button-down dress code. In addition, the political culture of the organization is much more conservative than your own.

There are four avenues you may follow:

1. You decide that you will not be accepted no matter what you do. You will seek employment elsewhere and leave when you get another job offer.
2. You remain in the organization but decide not to change your style to fit the organization.
3. You adapt totally to the organization's culture, values, and politics.
4. You learn to adapt to the organization's culture while maintaining your own sense of identity. You go as far as you can to fit in without giving up your core values and political views.

Number one, number two, and number three are extreme positions. Number one is deciding there is no hope for you. With all your attempts at accommodation, you feel the organization is too rigid and that you will never make it. Number two's position is that you cannot or will not change. Ultimately, this will probably lead to dissatisfaction on your part and on the part of the organization. Number three denotes total assimilation, accommodation, or "selling out."

Number four implies mutual accommodation between yourself and the organization. A Mexican-American woman said, " I am not assimilating, but acculturating to the organization. I see myself as a change agent. I wear my traditional business suit, but sometimes I wear a Mexican blouse with it or wear silver ethnic jewelry. On the language issue I'm emphatic. Of course I don't speak Spanish much on the job, but now and then I drop a few phrases to connect with other Latinos and to remind others who I am. I will not totally give up my Spanish. I'm proud of being bilingual and feel the company should prize this important skill that I bring." An African-American woman said, "Some blacks think that 'acting like whites' is giving up their identity, but successful blacks see it as 'adding on' something to their identity, not losing it."

The willingness to conform—to give up some independence—is a part of organizational life even if you are a white male and a member of the dominant culture. What you can or cannot give up in terms of your culture is an individual decision. What you can or cannot give up of your culture is also an issue of organizational reality and must be tested, case by case.

Let's look now at several case studies. Did the workers described in the following scenes "buy in" or did they "sell out"?

Scenes from the Workplace

WINNING THE GAME?

Catherine Pierce is the envy of the town. She apparently has it all—a great job, a wonderful family with three successful grown children, and a supportive husband. Now forty-eight, Catherine is taking an inventory of her life because she is being interviewed next month by the local newspaper. She will be the feature story in the Sunday magazine section. Needless to say she is excited, although anxious, about the interview.

Currently, Catherine is the senior vice president of a major bank. An Ivy League graduate with an MBA, Catherine has risen to the top of her field. Her rise to this position has not been without sacrifice. As a black woman, she has been ridiculed because of her personal choices. Prophetically, there was her choice to attend a mostly "white" undergraduate college instead of the "black" college to which her friends were going. Then, upon graduation, instead of joining her friends for a united graduation celebration, she decided to hold her own at home.

Unfortunately, it was on the same night as her neighborhood friends' party—so her only attendees were her white college friends.

At her party she announced that she would be attending the University of Pennsylvania's Wharton School in the fall. She also announced her engagement to her high school and neighborhood sweetheart. The night was not without other surprises, though. Her neighborhood black friends decided to surprise her by bringing their party to Catherine's house. A culture clash began. The food, the music, the dancing, the conversation, the entire attitude of the party was changed in an instant. Within forty minutes of the arrival of her black friends, her white friends made excuses and left. It was indeed a night to forget.

Catherine was hired by her current employer, a local bank, upon graduation from Wharton. She fully expected this to be just a steppingstone job. However, her successes landed her on several key task forces for the bank. Within eight years the bank acquired four additional banks. The local bank was now playing with the big boys, and so was she.

Slowly, Catherine began to assume the behavior of her white male counterparts. She gave up her inclusive style of management to become more authoritative. She frequently found herself engaged in "devil's advocate" behaviors, behaviors once reserved for the "good old boys." Moreover, her criticism of her peers became more forceful; she never revealed any uncertainties and was adept at the pastime of "bantering."

In her thirteenth year at the bank, she divorced her high school sweetheart and was remarried, this time to a white man. She immediately moved to an exclusive white neighborhood and dropped many of her black friends. Her taste in music changed, her active participation in the NAACP and other minority organizations came to a halt, and her activity in the 100 Black Women organization was limited to small monetary contributions.

Her career continued to grow, even when her "local" bank was acquired by one of the nation's largest banks. She survived the merger and was given a high-level position in the parent bank. Her career was made.

But at what cost? Not only had she lost her connections with the black community, but she had given up a supportive and participatory leadership style that had once been more natural for her as a woman. She consciously adopted the behavior of the white male–dominated workplace—and it resulted in career success!

She is reflecting on this now because she knows that the reporter, who is African-American, is interested in determining if she is in fact a "sellout" or a role model. As of this moment, Catherine herself is unsure: unsure because she found herself missing some of the essential parts of her life, some of her ethnic and gender tendencies; unsure because she, in her private moments, wonders if she could have succeeded if she had been "herself"; unsure because she is not certain who she is at all. Will this reporter criticize her, as had every other black person she'd met recently, or would she admire her because of the success she'd gained in spite of being a woman and being black? Catherine decides that her life is worthwhile and successful and that she will not apologize for figuring out the game and winning at it. After all, she surmises, why play the game if not to win—and she had won the game. Right?

What Should Catherine Have Done?

There are at least four possible approaches to this case, as follows:

1. Did Catherine totally sell out? If she did, is there anything wrong with this if the outcome is her own success and her ability to be a pioneer and a role model to other black women who want to make it in the dominant white culture?
2. Could she have succeeded by playing the game, changing her business persona *completely* to meet the dominant culture's criteria, but still maintaining her basic sense of self? Could Catherine have successfully separated her business persona from her private persona? Could she have kept her black friends, lived in an integrated neighborhood, and actively supported black charities?
3. Could she have succeeded by *partially* amending her behavior to meet the corporation where it was without totally selling out? Did she have to behave at the extreme of organizational culture? Rather, could she have just made subtle movements toward the corporate cultural norms without losing her natural leadership style, which was perhaps more inclusive than the style of most white males? As an African-American, did she have to whitewash everything in her personal style that would be perceived as "black?"

4. Could Catherine have succeeded if she hadn't played the game at all? And if she'd failed to reach the heights, would that have been okay?

What Most Women of Color Do to Succeed

Successful black women we have interviewed felt, sadly, that they had to give up some of their culture on the job. When questioned more deeply, most women of color said they had not given up *all* of their identity and their culture. It was a matter of definition and degree. At work they met the stylistic demands of their organization; at home, they reverted for the most part to their culture as women and African-Americans. The demands of their nurturing roles as mothers or caregivers were rarely discussed at the workplace. Another difference from Catherine's approach was that they never forgot where they came from, and they made a conscious effort to ally themselves with their cultural group, person-to-person and in black organizations. They also felt an obligation to "bring others of their cultural group along with them." They saw themselves as pioneers or role models. But some sadness remained for most.

Most black women, however they defined their level of success, would agree that amending their behavior, rather than completely giving up their cultural style, is the first step. And, for many, the good news was that they did not have to behave at the extreme of corporate culture. Rather, just making subtle movements toward the corporate cultural norms was their strategy. They then found that, by slight modification of their style, the organization was more accepting of them—for themselves.

"We have always lived in two worlds," said a prominent black female executive. And scores of black males that we interviewed agreed. "It's just natural for us to do that," said a black medical director.

SPEAKING SPANISH ON THE JOB

Maria Cabreras is a Cuban-American administrative assistant in a health maintenance organization. She is ambitious in her career plans and attends college at night, working toward a BA. She was born in the United States, but her parents speak Spanish in the home, and she lives in an area where most people are bilingual. Like many other Latinos, she feels that speaking Spanish has a special meaning for her—it affirms an important part of her identity and provides an emotional connection to other people who have a similar cultural heritage. Also, she is proud of the fact that she is bilingual.

In her job, she speaks English most of the time—to her boss, to clients of the organization, and to fellow workers.

Maria is a very friendly person and feels that her work relationships are very important to her. Indeed, she thinks of many of her co-workers as almost like "family." She chats easily with people and generally knows something about the families and outside interests of several of her co-workers. When she is near other Latinos, in her department or others, Maria often greets them in Spanish. Sometimes she speaks briefly; at other times, she talks at length in Spanish.

When she speaks at length in Spanish, it often has to do with a work project. She feels she can communicate more clearly to some of her Latino co-workers in Spanish, making subtle interpretations that sometimes elude her when using English. In addition, she is concerned that if she speaks only in English to them, they might think she is trying to be too "Anglo." She was once accused of denying her heritage because she did not speak in Spanish to someone at work.

Maria's boss, Sonia Olin, is pleased with Maria's work but is annoyed when Maria speaks Spanish on the job. She has spoken to Maria several times about this and recently tells her, very clearly and emphatically, that she does not want Maria to speak Spanish to co-workers while she is on the job.

Maria objects and says, "Sonia, you just don't understand. My fellow Latino workers are like family to me. I can't reject them by speaking only in English. Speaking Spanish to my Latino colleagues is extremely important to me."

What Should Maria Have Done?

Maria should have done the following:

1. Maria had to recognize that she has two loyalties—to her Latino heritage and to her work. She had to clarify for herself how she could remain loyal to both, maintaining good relationships with

Latino colleagues and with non-Spanish-speaking colleagues as well. That was her challenge—how to "buy in" but not "sell out."

2. She should have realized that many people feel excluded when someone speaks in a language that they do not understand. Some people feel that the non-English-speaking person is talking about them behind their backs. Other people think that it is simply rude; they feel excluded from office talk conducted in a language other than English. Some simply object "on principle." "This is America," some say. "You should speak English here." And then there are some, but certainly not all, who may simply be prejudiced against Latinos. (Remember from our first strategy, "Check Your Baggage"—don't assume that everyone is hostile.)
3. Although court decisions have affirmed the right to speak foreign languages on the job if it does not interfere with job performance, Maria should have realized that speaking Spanish can cause problems in the workplace, as indicated above, and will certainly be a barrier to her career progress if she continues speaking Spanish on the job as much as she has.
4. Maria should have told Sonia why speaking Spanish is so important to her. Maria should have agreed to limit—but not totally eliminate—Spanish on the job when other people are around and to try speaking Spanish only in social situations—like at lunch or while on a break.
5. Just as she prided herself on her friendliness to Latino colleagues, Maria should have attempted to develop friendships with non-Latino co-workers as well. Doing so would have broadened her perspective and her network throughout the organization and helped her to be seen as a larger player in the company. She should have been aware that others, whom she may need in order to advance in the company, may be turned off because of her Spanish conversations, which seem to shut them out. Maria needed *all* the help she could get from everyone in the organization, and she should have done what was necessary to reach out for that help.
6. She should have explained to her Latino colleagues that she is, of course, proud of her heritage, that she values her relationships with Latino co-workers and friends and is in no way rejecting them, but she wants to expand to a larger world, to have relation-

ships with Latinos but also with other workers in the organization. She should have explained that she wanted to progress in her career and knew that speaking less Spanish was the way. She was not choosing between her Latino colleagues and the "Anglos." She wanted to be included in *both* worlds on the job and refused to be limited to choosing between them.

What Might Maria Have Said to Sonia, Her Boss?

Maria might have said the following: "Sonia, I want you to know that my language is very important to me, as it is to many Latinos. It connects us to others of the same heritage. But in no way do I mean to exclude other people from those of us who speak Spanish. I agree that it will be a good idea for me—and others—to limit speaking Spanish to social periods, such as breaks and lunches, for example.

"Although I do make an effort to be friendly and connect to most people in the department, regardless of background, I am going to try to make an effort to be more involved in organizational activities.

"As you know, I am working on my degree, and would like to stay in this health maintenance organization. I would really appreciate any help you can give me toward advancing my career as I finish my degree."

What Might Maria Have Said to Latino Colleagues Who Address Her in Spanish?

Maria might have said the following: "Luis, I want you to know that I'm going to try to limit speaking Spanish in the office. That doesn't mean that we can't say hello or chat in the cafeteria or after work. But I don't want to be pigeon-holed in the company as being only Latino; I honestly believe that will limit my career chances. I hope you can understand my position. I'm as proud of my heritage as anyone. You know how active I am in our local church and the neighborhood Latino organization. Of course, I will continue to do that. But I also want to get ahead for the good of myself and my family."

ACCOMMODATING COMMUNICATION STYLE: CAN IT AND SHOULD IT BE DONE?

Robert Oliver is a black senior sales trainer for a large computer manufacturing company, a job he has held for six months. He previously had an excellent record in sales and as a sales trainer and was asked to head up a new regional training unit to get it off the ground. Robert has great enthusiasm and a reputation as a real go-getter. His style in training is assertive and challenging. He relates that he developed his skills in the ghetto, where you would be crushed if you showed any weakness. His style is now a reflection of his character. His feedback to his trainees is "blunt and honest," as he himself would say. In fact, Robert takes pride in "telling it like it is." When asked about his style, he says, "Anyone in sales has to be tough. I know my people can take it. They'd better get used to the real world out there."

Several of the trainees have objected to the way Robert has challenged them in class. They think he is too rough and confrontational in the way he gives feedback. Although Robert has offered to speak after class to anyone who wants additional assistance, several of the unhappy trainees don't speak to him about their concerns but instead go to his boss, the director of sales, to complain. They say that Robert is "too aggressive and angry and has a chip on his shoulder."

Alan Watson, the director of sales, is new to his job. Although he had heard some good things about Robert before coming to the department, he really didn't know much about his excellent reputation. Moreover, he had never worked with a black manager as senior as Robert.

Alan calls Robert in and tells him that he is antagonizing some of the trainees and that he should "tone his communication style down." "I don't know about how you worked with the previous director," he continues, "but it seems to me that your style is too strong and confrontational. I don't want to hear any more complaints from the sales reps. I hope you'll be able to work it out and do it the way I like things done here."

Robert thinks: "Here we go again. I had this great reputation at my last job, and now I have to start all over again. As an African-American your reputation doesn't travel with you. You have to prove yourself all over again. I know if I were white my style would be seen as an asset, especially in sales. What's seen as anger in me is seen as strength in a white guy."

What Should Robert Have Done?

Robert should have done the following:

1. This scenario calls for clear communication and mutual accommodation between the boss and Robert. Since Robert's reputation as

a salesman and sales trainer was not known to Alan, it was imperative for Robert to discuss his record of excellence in view of the trainees' complaints about him. Robert should have asked Alan to be more definitive about what the charges were against him. How many people were there who complained about him? What was their background and experience? Perhaps only two or three trainees objected to his style, and perhaps they objected because of regional or cultural differences.

2. Robert should have asked Alan for feedback on how he might explain his style to those not used to his manner. He might have reviewed, with Alan, the benefits of his assertive and forceful feedback style and invited him to sit in on the training to observe him.
3. If his boss, Alan, upon observing him, suggested that Robert modify his confrontational manner of training, Robert should have discussed his hesitancy in radically changing his training style in view of his excellent record with the same style. Robert, however, could also have assured his boss that he would modify his style somewhat, where appropriate, softening his feedback to trainees and modifying some verbiage that might be misunderstood by others. Robert should have asked for Alan's support when trainees go over his head to speak to Alan. He should have requested that Alan tell the trainees to speak to Robert directly about any of their concerns.

What Might Robert Have Said to Alan, His Boss?

Robert might have said the following: "Alan, I'm concerned that two of the trainees complained to you about my training style, which they seem to think is too tough. I'm upset for two reasons: (1) my style, which has proved so successful in the past, is now seen in this company as detrimental, and (2) the trainees went directly to you without speaking to me first. I'd like you to sit in on one of my training sessions to give me feedback on my training style. I'd like *specific* feedback on what exactly it is in my manner or verbiage that may be seen as too confrontational. I also need your help in explaining my style to those trainees who misunderstand my intent and are uncomfortable with my manner.

"It's very hard to change a communication style, particularly when it has proven so successful in the past. However, if there is some modification needed in my manner that doesn't affect my basic identity, I will willingly adapt to trainees' needs. But we need feedback from more of the class, because two or three trainees' reactions doesn't mean that the whole class is negative. I would like to work this out so that the benefit of my assertive style for sales is appreciated and that, with minor adaptations, I can lessen trainees' complaints. I welcome your help in doing this."

What Might Robert Have Said to Either the Whole Class or to Those Who Have Complained About Him?

Robert might have said the following: "I want to talk to you about my training style, which is sometimes misunderstood. Some of you may think I'm too confrontational when I give you feedback, and that I'm too critical. I have no intention of being harsh. I was hired for this job because of my record of success in sales and as a trainer. Therefore, I see no need to change my manner or style in any fundamental way. If you have any problem or concern, please come directly to me, and we can talk about my feedback style and your interpretation of it. I want to assure you that I am very pleased with the way this group is doing, and all of you have the potential for significant success."

WHY IS MY INTERPERSONAL STYLE MISCONSTRUED? IT'S JUST CULTURAL

Don Lopez, a Puerto Rican senior manager in a large bank, is confused—and more. He is angry. What has happened to the workplace where for nine years he has been so content? He knows he is respected and admired for his competence and his interpersonal skills. He supervises a staff of six women and has been known to be very fair to them.

Don is very warm and affectionate, which is as much a result of his upbringing as it is of his inherent personality. For example, everyone in his family hugs each other when they meet. In his culture, people are generous with compliments. Don, a smart dresser himself, admires a well-groomed person and lets him or her know it. His behavior is no different in the workplace.

To Don's shock and dismay, he is called into the Human Resources

Department to hear that Marna Gardener, a recently hired staff member, has complained about Don's behavior. Marna is accusing him of sexual harassment, complaining that he makes inappropriate remarks about her appearance and even puts his arm around her on occasions. She also resents his habit of sitting on the desks of the other women, laughing and making casual jokes about the women's social lives.

Celine Barton, the human resources manager, tells Don that he must modify his interpersonal style with his staff. He is also told that touching, even though it is meant as a warm and friendly gesture, can be misinterpreted and that telling jokes with sexual connotations is offensive to some people, and certainly inappropriate in an office setting. Celine reminds him that the company is very aware now about the liabilities concerning sexual harassment. He is told to review the employee manual covering sexual harassment and to be more circumspect in his behavior. This includes avoiding personal comments about appearance. Nothing will be put in his record at this time, but he is being warned.

Don's mood ranges from humiliation to disbelief. "Is this what the workplace is coming to?" he thinks. "Grim, cold, humorless. I'm happily married, a father of three daughters. I'm not sexually harassing anyone. I don't want to 'make out.' I want to 'make it'—be considered for an executive position. Now am I to be branded and condemned for my interpersonal skills, which have served me so well in the past? Have I ruined my chances for success? I was raised in a culture that prides itself on warmth and good interpersonal relations. Do I have to give up my heritage? What do I think or do now?"

What Should Don Have Done?

Don should have done the following:

1. Don should have realized that a new workplace reality requires more sensitivity about behavior—verbal and nonverbal—that can have sexual overtones. Organizational guidelines for avoiding charges of sexual harassment suggest that people avoid commenting on other people's appearance except in a general way. Remarks about someone's body or sexual attractiveness or jokes that have sexual innuendoes can be misinterpreted and may be offensive to some people.

2. There is a new sensitivity about sexual harassment that Don should have known about, particularly as a supervisor. He should have been aware of his potential liability regarding sexual harassment. This does not mean that he cannot compliment someone or be friendly—not at all. He had to realize, however, that there is a difference between (a) remarks and jokes that have sexual connotations and casual touching and hugging and (b) behavior that is simply friendly. While Don felt that his behavior was intended to be only friendly, he should have understood that *intention* is not what matters but the *impact* the behavior has on others. Thus, people from certain ethnic or religious backgrounds may find any touching or any conversations with sexual connotations offensive.
3. Don needed to know that he did not have to give up the important and valuable aspect of Latino culture called *personalismo*. This Latino cultural tendency does not have to include anything sexual. Bonding and personal relationships can be developed based on shared interests in food, holidays, children, family, current events, work, and the like. There is a wide area of relationships that do not have a sexual dimension.

What Might Don Have Said to Celine, the Human Resources Manager?

Don might have said the following: "Celine, I didn't realize that my jokes, comments, or any part of my behavior was offensive to Marna. I certainly did not—and do not—want to offend her in any way. As you know, I am a very friendly person and like to create a family-like work atmosphere. This has always worked well in the past—as least as far as I know. But if Marna or maybe others object or see things differently, of course I'm going to change. The sexual harassment charge is serious enough to make me more conscious of my actions and how they may be perceived by others.

"However, I am determined to keep up an informal, friendly atmosphere in my work unit. The challenge for me now is to adapt my style so that it is not offensive to anyone. I'm not going to go so overboard that we can't compliment each other or kid around in general ways, but I realize that I have to strike the right balance."

What Might Don Say to Marna, the Staff Member?

Don might say the following: "I'm sorry that at times my behavior has offended you. I had no intention of doing so. Let me assure you that I want to work together with you and all the staff in a professional and respectful way. If at any time in the future you feel my friendliness has crossed the line, please let me know."

Listen to some people who were successful in "buying into" the organization without "selling out."

SUCCESS STORIES

"IT TAKES TIME TO BE ACCEPTED"

Helene Doring is a copywriter manager in an advertising company. She said, "I am a lesbian, and even when I felt it was okay to 'come out' because I had proven myself through my superior performance, I still compromised on basic issues. At company picnics I felt paranoid because I thought everyone was curious about my behavior and wondered whether I would show outward displays of affection toward my life partner. I realized that there were double standards, that everyone else could show affection toward their mate, but for me it was taboo. So I went along with that taboo.

"But it's interesting. Over time, when others got to know us, we became more accepted by the group. I guess everyone realized that we were not such freaks, and that our relationship was as real and important to me as theirs was to them. I realize that first you have to meet people where they are before they can accept you for what you are. You have to realize others' discomfort. It takes time, but it's worth it. Moreover, my career has not faltered one bit. I still get plum assignments and still get chewed out when I screw up—just like everyone else."

• — •

MAXIMIZING YOURSELF IS NOT SELLING OUT

"As the only high-ranking Latino male in an Internet company, I had much to adapt to," said Julio Sanchez. "I learned how to be cross-cultural, to know the organization's culture, to read people. I tried to understand people and find out what is the most effective posture to take. For the first few months on the job I listened, looked, kept quiet, and found out who has the power.

" 'Buying in' means not going into the retreat mode; you've got to be out there. I got into networks, joined organizational groups. If you're seen as a person with your nose only to the grindstone, you give the aura of separation or coolness.

"I bought in by fighting the stereotypes and perceptions of others. I know this is a minority problem—downplaying yourself. I bought in by selling myself, which is not what most Latinos do. So many of us play ourselves down. And so many Latinos are seen as easygoing and laid-back. I overcame that perception; I talked and let my ideas out. And I grabbed opportunities. This is not typical of our culture.

"I knew my strong accent was a detriment to my career so I perfected my language skills through classes. I didn't see this as selling out; I saw it as a practical matter of making myself better understood. Working on my language skills was especially important to me because I was the only Latino in a management position and very aware that no one else looked like me.

"One of my cultural strengths is that I know the ways to work with people as a team. My easygoing nature is an asset in developing relationships. I am available to help others, and that skill soon became apparent.

"I overcame my language problem and learned to speak up for myself. I was assertive in asking for additional work; I told my supervisor that I am qualified to manage people. I asked for a job with more responsibility, but I made sure that there was no ethnicity in the title. As manager for special markets, I insisted that the title be changed to products manager.

"Yes, I 'bought in,' but there are issues on which I won't 'sell out.' I have seen others who pronounce their name differently, who never are caught in a Latino group, who play down their ethnicity. I don't do that. Whatever challenges I faced, I never forgot where I came from and the strength of the values that my heritage has given me."

"I PUT DOWN MY STAKES—THE LINE THAT I DRAW"

"I am one of the few blacks and the top-ranking black female in my accounting and consulting firm," said Eleanor Graves, now fifty-five years old. "I have risen in the firm to the position of managing director, against many odds, external and internal. External odds, because I had no mentor, female or black. Internal, because I had to make a decision to ignore or pass over questionable slights from my co-workers and bosses. Even harder for me was the fact that, for many of my black friends, I'm a 'sellout' because I work in a firm where I appear to be a 'token.' I see it differently; I'm pulling up other people of color who are entering the firm. I had no help, but I can help *them* rise.

"I made it—yes, alone—because I had decided to focus totally on my work and the positive experiences I usually have. I'm very low-key, and I pride myself on getting along with most people. I determined not to have a chip on my shoulder. I deliberately tried to overcome the stereotypes people have of blacks; I will not play into it.

"Whether or not to adapt to the norms of the organization is a choice everyone has to make. But most people switch their behavior to adapt to the expected norm. Blacks are constantly 'code-switching'—intuitively knowing how to adapt to others' expectations. We do it automatically, as do other 'minorities'; it's only white males who can stay constant. Everyone else must try to adapt to the white model of proper or accepted decorum. I made that choice, even if I hate it, because I know that fitting in is an important part of how the organization judges your so-called interpersonal style.

"I may have bought into the organizational style of behavior, but I have also defined for myself the line that I draw. I put down the stakes. In other words, I won't let people go beyond a certain point in their negative remarks. Maybe my stakes are drawn closer in than other blacks'. I try to clarify the remarks in a nonjudgmental way, let some remarks go, deflect the conversation, or just walk away. Other blacks in the workplace will get angry on the spot and make an issue over any behavior that they think is prejudicial or stereotypical.

"I have bought in to the American dream of success. I know who I am, a proud black woman who picks and chooses my battles very carefully. Success is the best revenge against those who want to put me—or other blacks—down."

FITTING CULTURAL VALUES TO THE JOB

As a director of the social services department in a large city hospital, Irene Chu realized that few Asian-Americans, especially women, held her level of executive position.

"I was born in Taiwan and come from a very traditional Chinese family, but I was raised in the United States. I have struggled and succeeded in overcoming barriers faced by many Asian-Americans. Maybe because I have been trained as a clinical social worker, I have some insights into my success that others might not have.

"First, I had to become aware of how my traditional values affected my behavior at work. At first, I saw my supervisors as representing authority, like my parents in the home. I had to learn that it was okay to speak up, on the job, to authority figures, even when I still didn't feel comfortable doing so at home. Sounds obvious, doesn't it? But it takes getting used to the fact that dealing with people at work is not the same as with family members at home.

"Another thing I overcame was self-blame. Many Asians are driven by this. We don't always deal well with criticism. When my supervisors said something vaguely critical, I thought, 'I should have done better. I should have known that. I didn't do well enough.' Shame was always prevalent. Fortunately, I had some colleagues and supervisors—Asians and others—who continually gave me reality checks. I learned to ask myself: 'Did I really have enough time, support, advice, and information to do the job differently?' Sometimes, it was my fault. But, more often, there was a legitimate explanation for my actions. Realizing this helped build my self-confidence. I learned not to be defensive when confronted with some unusual supervisors. For example, whenever I went to one particular supervisor for some minor information or just to 'touch base' (which I later learned was seen as not taking enough initiative), this supervisor barraged me with questions. 'Why, why, why?' was how I experienced her many questions. I felt that she was intrusive and critical, that she was implicitly asking me, 'How come you didn't do this or that?'

"When I realized my problem in dealing with this supervisor, I decided to modify my approach. I gave her background information on what I was doing, offered several alternative plans, and then asked for her advice or concurrence on what I thought was the best plan.

"What was helpful to me was to distance myself—separate myself from a situation when analyzing it. I looked for patterns in my behavior. 'Do I always react this way when someone questions me or criticizes me?' If I feel paralyzed in a situation, I realize that it is usually part of my past or a cultural experience that comes into play. In situations like that, I try to pretend I am another person and see how that person would advise me on how to deal with the problem.

"I recognize that I have something valuable to offer—both in my work and in some aspects of my style. Like many Asians, I am well disciplined and tend to contain aggression and not to express negative feelings. I will avoid direct conflict in a staff meeting. But I use that cultural trait to my advantage. I contain the aggression from others, then deliberate back in my office and get back to people with a well-developed response when tempers have cooled. I see this as an advantage. I modified a cultural characteristic and made it a positive for dealing with conflict.

"I had supervisors in the past who felt I was unable to deal directly with conflict—they saw this as a weakness. But I explained that my style of handling conflict was different from theirs and that I wasn't avoiding the conflict but simply dealing with it in a different way. For the most part, this was accepted. By explaining myself to others, with confidence, and being comfortable with my own style instead of simply trying to imitate others, I was seen as a potential leader. And that's how I was finally able to assume the leadership of the department myself.

"Have I 'sold out' by redefining my cultural style for myself and for others? No, but I *have* adapted my cultural style to the norms of the organization, which had misinterpreted my leadership style and my ways of dealing with authority and conflict."

"I PACKAGED MYSELF TO APPEAL TO THE MARKET"

Roger Jackson, an African-American senior-level executive of a consumer electronics company, says, "To be successful in today's business environment you must be willing to adapt to the environment. You have to consider yourself a product. That's what I did. Just as I would do market research to discover what was needed in the marketplace and design the product to fit the needs of the market, I handled myself that same way. I figured I was the most important product I would ever sell. I packaged myself in a way that is appealing to the market, in this case to the senior-level executives in the organization. Does this mean I have 'sold out'?

"Hell, no. I still look in the mirror every day and realize that I am black, and that fact will never change. I still enjoy my sports, my jazz, and black women. True, I dress in a more conservative manner, but that is as much a product and influence of my mom as it is of any corporate pressure to conform. We African-Americans must lose this notion that if you can speak the King's English well, articulate your words and dress in a conservative Brooks Brothers suit, somehow you are not a brother, not black anymore. That's ridiculous! We come in a variety of shapes, sizes, shades of blackness, and intellectual capacity. But the bottom line is that we are all still black."

"BUYING IN" REQUIRES NEGOTIATION SKILLS

Obviously, Roger and the other "voices" we heard feel strongly about the fact that their core values are intact, regardless of their modifications of behavior or appearance and their attempts to accept people "where they are." Unfortunately, this is a point of concern for many people of color or of difference. Sometimes the pressure from their own community is so intense that they abandon their "marketing" plan for themselves. Remember Eleanor Graves, a top executive who had a struggle with friends who thought she might be selling out by staying in a company where she was the only person of color in a very senior position.

It's your choice, and yours alone, whether or not you want to change your behavior or attitudes to meet the norms of your organization. Too often, the choice is seen as "yes" or "no" to people who are not members of the dominant group; the idea of negotiation is overlooked or downplayed. This is because of insecurity on the job or because of cultural tendencies that prevent people from "demanding" something from a superior.

Successful employees from the dominant group have always known how to negotiate their differences with their bosses. If they want changes in their assignments, work schedules, or even the location of their offices, they feel comfortable in discussing their needs. They know that sometimes their requests will be accommodated and sometimes they will not. But successful employees ask for what they want and feel free to negotiate with their bosses.

Unfortunately, many people, even if they finally overcome a cultural reluctance to request accommodation, are not skillful in how they do it. Or sometimes, no matter how hard they try to negotiate, the organization is too rigid to change. The question for each individual is, "Was I skillful enough in my negotiation technique or is this organization so rigid or prejudiced that I won't be accommodated no matter what I do?"

Here are some areas for negotiation that will help enhance opportunities for advancement or a better working environment:

- Flexible hours for parents or caregivers
- Assignments that offer opportunities for growth instead of dead-end ethnic tracking
- Training that will provide "line" experience
- Time off for professional conferences
- Permission to decorate workspace with ethnic flair
- Inclusion in decision-making meetings (particularly for women and persons of color)
- Insistence on a job title that does not imply "special ethnic markets"
- Mentoring and ongoing feedback on career mobility and time frames for promotion
- Permission to wear Afrocentric hairstyle or display other ethnic stylistic differences
- Inclusion in the informal network
- Preventing offensive, stereotypical remarks about your group

When you are asking for something that is really important to you and your sense of identity in the workplace, keep in mind the following:

1. Reasonable people will differ. How you handle those differences can make or break your career path. Some employees who are in a minority in their organization feel that management deliberately puts them in stressful situations just to see how they will handle themselves. Sometimes this may be the case, but often it is not. (Review Strategy 1, "Check Your Baggage.") Unfortunately, what does seem to be true is that when people who are not of the dominant culture make a request or a demand for change, they are sometimes viewed as troublemakers.

This makes it especially important to find ways to resolve differences constructively.

An example of successful negotiation is that of Harry Clark, a black production manager in the training department of a large publications organization. His company had assigned him to head a summer internship program for minority college students. At the end of the summer, the company decided to provide a farewell dinner and tickets to a Broadway show to the interns. Neal Leaman, the head of the Human Resources Department, suggested that the group be taken to "Showboat," a Broadway hit. He thought it would be a special treat because tickets were expensive and hard to get.

When Harry told the interns about the choice, they were disappointed. Most of them said they would rather see "Jelly's Last Jam" or "Smokey Joe's Café," shows that featured black performers and involved stories about jazz. Several said they didn't like "Showboat." Some said it was too "old-fashioned." Some said they thought it showed blacks in a negative light.

When Harry told Neal about the interns' reaction, he seemed annoyed and uncomfortable. He didn't want to send the interns to a "black" show; he thought some people in the organization might think he was stereotyping the group. Harry explained that he understood the concerns and thought it was sensitive of Neal not to assume that the black interns would automatically want to see a "black" show. He explained that the interns were young and that some were not from New York and rarely had a chance to see a show; others from New York usually couldn't afford tickets. Because this was their only show, they preferred seeing something they knew they would enjoy.

Harry was able to successfully negotiate and explain to Neal the rationale for the interns' choice while at the same time expressing appreciation to the human resources manager for understanding the interns' perspective. He was "buying in" to Neal's best intentions but not "selling out" on the preference of the black interns for their choice of entertainment.

2. There are two ways people deal with conflict: emotionally or rationally. When feelings are running high, rational problem solving and reasonable discussion are very difficult for many people. However, most white men of the dominant workplace culture have been socialized *not* to show emotions and to handle conflict rationally. To be effective you

must adopt, as much as possible, this communication style of rationality. Otherwise, you run the risk of being labeled as an "angry" person, or a malcontent.

3. An essential key to effective resolution of conflict and differences is to temper your anger and emotion and to use some of the following steps in negotiating your needs:

- Treat the other person with respect.
- Listen until you understand the other person's point of view.
- Assertively state both your feelings and needs.
- Have a "fallback" position in mind.
- Keep all your options open.

4. Put yourself in the other person's place. Why should that person concede to your position? What's the benefit and cost to that individual? What arguments on the benefits and costs should make your request look beneficial to the boss and to the organization as a whole—as well as to you personally?

Example (a woman employee requesting flex time): "Jim, I'd like to suggest a change in my work schedule that will allow me to be less pressured and more creative in my work. It won't affect the other people in the unit because my work is done pretty much on my own and I can coordinate with other staff during our overlapping hours. This flexibility will allow me to be available to my school-age children in case of illness or special events. How do you think we can make this work successfully for all concerned? I know this company is committed to maximizing the productivity of its work teams and providing quality employment for everyone."

5. Make your argument at a convenient time; allow time for discussion.

Example (a Latino employee requesting other assignments): "Carol, what would be a convenient time for us to meet for about a half hour? I'd like to discuss other assignments for me that would enhance my skills and my opportunities in the company. I have so many ideas for where I can make a substantial contribution to the company that are not limited to the 'ethnic market' where I am now placed. This would also help our company fulfill its commitment to diversity."

6. Put a positive spin on your request.

Example (a black employee requesting permission to decorate his office): "Pete, I'd like to talk to you about the department's policy on decorating offices. I want to show you a new tapestry I got from my uncle in the Sudan that I'd like to hang in my office. I think it enhances our company's interest in making a statement about diversity. We might want to reconsider our policy against displaying ethnic art."

7. Prepare thoroughly for your negotiation, using the following steps:

- Identify and define the issue causing the conflict, acknowledging the interests of all parties.
- Identify areas of agreement.
- Isolate the areas of difference.
- Invite and offer all options for a resolution to the conflict.
- Agree on a solution and mutual action steps, including a process for evaluating the effectiveness of the resolution.

In their classic work on negotiation, *Getting to Yes*, Roger Fisher and William Ury emphasize the absolute necessity of knowing the difference between *positions* and *interests*. For example, the female worker who requests flexible hours may take the *position* that she cannot work a 9-to-5 schedule. The boss may take the *position* that it is not possible to adjust her hours. But what are the *interests and needs* of both parties? The *interests and needs* of the woman who wants flexible hours are that she has to be available for her children at certain hours.

The *interests and needs* of the boss may be the need to have the office covered at all times and the fear of setting a precedent for other workers. Both parties would be more successful if they addressed the *interests or needs* of the other, rather than their stated *positions*.

While all of these points seem reasonable on the printed page, they may be extremely difficult when they have to be applied. Some people may find it difficult to be assertive in expressing their own needs and feelings; others may find it difficult to listen and be respectful when they are certain that they or their group has been offended. This latter issue of responding to what may be a discriminatory remark is surely one of the most sensitive and controversial issues in interpersonal relationships.

What do you do when you hear a discriminatory remark about your group or about other groups? Are you selling out if you ignore these negative remarks even if they are sometimes said in jest? Not necessarily.

Here are some examples of stereotypic and prejudicial remarks:

- "What do you people really want? Do all blacks expect to go to Harvard?"
- "*Mañana, mañana*. You people are never on time."
- (To a man): "Oh, he's as queer as a three-dollar bill." (To a woman): "Got to hand it to you, kid. You're a ball breaker."

Practicing is one effective strategy in responding to a negative stereotype. You might respond in one of the following ways, depending on who made the remark—your boss, your peer, or a person you considered a friend:

An African-American senior executive said, "I take people where they are. For example, to the remark, 'What do they all want?' I might say, 'What do you mean, *all*?' Or something like, 'Who wouldn't want to go to Harvard?' I would just deflect the remark, and not let it get to me. Sorry, I don't see it as selling out. But I'm going to pick and choose what I wish to confront."

"If I heard the remark, '*mañana, mañana*,' " a Latino male said, "to anyone but my boss I would answer, 'I'm sure you didn't mean that as an insult, but it could be taken that way. I can take a joke, but I want to give you a heads-up. Others might be offended by that remark, which lumps all Latinos together as not being responsible about time.' To my boss, I might say, 'I know a lot of Latinos who are always on time, if not early. You know I'm one of them.' "

To the 'queer as a three-dollar bill' remark, an appropriate retort could be, "I don't think the company would like that kind of remark, and personally I find the expression offensive too." "Coming from my boss," said a lesbian employee who is not out, "I would ignore the remark, but certainly not smile, or laugh."

To the "you're a ball breaker" remark, a woman might say, "You might mean that as a compliment. But I don't see it that way. I'd rather be thought of as a strong person." If it's about another woman, one might say, "I don't feel comfortable with that remark, and I think other women would find that offensive too. It implies that if women take a strong position they are hostile to men."

Have you heard the adage that 80 percent of communication is nonverbal? Do you remember that as a child you were told, "It's not what you say, it's how you say it"? Yes, this adage is right. Bear that in mind when you choose to reply. With the suggested remarks above, remember to keep your tone and facial expression neutral. Making a person defensive or guilty is not your goal. Nobody likes a self-righteous person, and you must avoid even the perception of that stance. You just want to state your position, neutrally, without casting any aspersions upon the speaker.

Lack of agreement or disapproval can be shown without words. Silence, with a slight raise of the eyebrows, or looking away can signify disagreement, or at least non-agreement. Not laughing at hurtful jokes carries its own message. However, if you act too disapproving or contemptuous, you might make the other person feel that they are racist or boorish and thereby cut off all further dialogue.

What is important to remember is that by carefully weighing your response, you are not necessarily "selling out." You are picking your battles, you are choosing to educate, you are taking people where they are, you are not assuming that everyone is hostile, and you are "checking your baggage" (see Strategy 1). You have neither validated nor agreed with discriminatory or insensitive remarks. This is one area in which you will never "buy in."

SUMMARY

STRATEGY 5: BUY IN, DON'T SELL OUT

1. Recognize your cultural characteristics and how these might be a barrier to your effectiveness in the organization.
2. Acknowledge those characteristics that you can't give up and those on which you are willing to compromise in order to "buy in" and adjust to the organizational culture.
3. Don't see every change or accommodation to the organization's culture as "giving up" or "giving in" but rather as a way of adapting

to a new and different situation. Some compromises are just that—compromises—but do not constitute "selling out."

4. Don't let others from your group define for you where to "draw the line." You have to decide this for yourself.
5. Learn how to handle offensive remarks about you, your group, or other groups. Containing your anger and dealing with the remarks rationally is not "selling out."
6. Learn how to negotiate for change that accommodates your special needs so that you don't feel that you are "selling out" to the organization.
7. If you feel that you cannot be "true to yourself," seek employment in an organization that is friendly to your needs. More and more companies are sensitive to diversity issues. Numerous books, magazines, and other publications list corporations and organizations that are known to be responsive to members of diverse groups. If you do choose to leave your current employment, don't do so by "burning your bridges" behind you, or before you have another job offer.

STRATEGY 

KNOW YOUR RIGHTS

And How to Get Them

Let's say you think you are being treated unfairly. You think that someone else got a job that you deserved. Your boss is supercritical and uses derogatory words with racial or gender references. Several co-workers display offensive or pornographic pictures in their work area and prominently show them to other staff members. What should you do?

First of all, you have to at least acknowledge to yourself that something is amiss and that you are not just imagining that something may be unfair in the way you are being treated or in the workplace atmosphere. Some people are not only in denial about their mistreatment but may blame themselves for what is happening. They blame only themselves if they don't get a promotion. If their boss yells at them, they think they must have deserved it. They are worried that others will think they are prudish and making too much out of material they find vulgar and offensive. Sometimes people aren't even aware that others, with the same seniority and accomplishments, are getting much higher pay.

At the other extreme, some people see every slight, every denied job opportunity or pay discrepancy as discriminatory and based exclusively on racism, sexism, ageism, or some other kind of prejudice. We examined some of these issues in our first strategy, "Check Your Baggage," and pointed out the importance of judging each case and each person individually before making a judgment about discrimination or prejudice.

Therefore, you must assess your situation carefully and dispassionately. If you are concerned about your salary or a promotion, you should have some notion of your value in the workplace based on your work performance, experience, evaluations, and educational background. Then you can evaluate your situation in relation to that of others whose performance and background are similar to yours. Try to find other people in the organization who can help you in this assessment. It is important for you to have the self-esteem and sense of your own worth to feel that you deserve to be treated with respect and recognized for your abilities. Of course, respectful treatment and recognition of ability is not always given in organizations. And you may not always be protected by law. But our purpose here is to help you realize that being treated fairly and knowing your rights should be your goal. You need to set this goal before you can develop a strategy for achieving what you think are your rights in the workplace. The unfairness might be the lack of a promotion, inability to get a job in a line position, pay inequity, sexual harassment, racial or ethnic slurs, or other forms of discrimination based on race, religion, ethnicity, sexual orientation, disability, or age.

If you feel that you are not being treated fairly, you then have to decide what you will do or not do. We suggest four stages to go through. To remember them, we are providing another acronym: SOAR.

S Self: Solving the unfairness on your own

O Organizational Remedies: Getting organizational procedures or organizational allies to work for you

A Actionable (legal rights): Taking legal action to remedy illegal discrimination

R Resign: Leaving for another job or resign yourself to staying because the benefits of staying outweigh the cost of leaving the job

Each of these stages will be discussed at length at the end of this strategy. You will have to decide which action or actions you are willing to take—and the consequences of each.

Can your one, lonely voice really make a difference? Will your "whistle blowing" behavior mark you and drive you further into the abyss? The remainder of this strategy will suggest some ways for you to recognize, decide, and act in situations of discrimination. We will explore some of the potential risks and benefits of these behaviors.

Let's look now at some workplace scenarios that illustrate how people typically cope with unfairness in the workplace, and how they could have used different strategies to be more successful.

Scenes from the Workplace

"Pregnant? Too Bad!"

Jean Linder is a mid-level manager at a manufacturing company, where she has worked for the past five years. With an excellent record of achievement in her job, she has no doubt that she will someday be promoted to a top executive position. In preparation for this position, she has recently earned a master's degree in chemistry.

Several months ago, she found out she was pregnant. She is reluctant to tell her boss, George Presto, the division head, because she knows of several other women who were eased out of their positions either before they gave birth or shortly after they returned to work.

At the end of a meeting with George about a new product, Jean mentions her pregnancy. She says she plans to work until a week before her delivery date and then take a three-month leave of absence. She begins describing the plans she has carefully worked out for distributing her work. George cuts her short and says, "I knew this was going to happen sooner or later—it always does with you gals." He says this as if a disaster were about to occur. "There's no point in talking about this now. We'll think about it later," George says and then rushes out of his office. Jean can tell that George is very annoyed about what he assumes is going to happen. She worries about the implications for her. "I think that legally this company has to guarantee my job, but I know that George can make it very rough for me."

Three weeks pass, and a choice assignment is taken away from Jean. And then an opportunity to attend a training conference that she had expected to attend is given to another manager. When she asks George about the assignment and training conference, he tells her, "Why bother worrying about it? Who knows how long you'll be out after the baby comes, or how much you want to kill yourself on this job?"

Jean is certain that her worst fears will be realized. Her career will be seriously sidetracked because of her pregnancy.

What Should Jean Have Done?

Jean should have done the following:

1. Jean has already taken the first step by realizing that something was wrong. George had taken away a key assignment and an opportunity to attend a training conference. Her ideas about distributing her work were ignored. In addition, he assumed that she would not work as hard after her return. Jean feels that she is experiencing discriminatory behavior already.
2. Jean should have known her rights under the Pregnancy Discrimination Act of 1979, which makes it illegal to discriminate on the basis of pregnancy, and the Family and Medical Leave Act of 1993. The latter grants employees in companies with fifty or more workers the right to take up to twelve weeks of unpaid leave for the birth of a child or the illness of a family member—and come back to their old jobs or at least to equivalent positions.
3. She should have spoken to George, her supervisor, and questioned him about his expressed concerns about her job performance now

and in the future. She should have reassured him about her commitment to productivity during her pregnancy and her determination to return to work three months after the birth of her child.

4. Jean could have reminded George, in a tactful—not blaming—way of the laws protecting her during pregnancy ("reasonable accommodation" if needed) and afterward. She should have assertively requested that she be allowed to go to the training conference and retain the assignment that was withdrawn from her. She should have provided George, in writing, with her suggested plan for distribution of work, as well as other contingency plans, during her leave of absence.
5. If Jean was not satisfied with George's response, she could have gone to the human resources, business ethics, or Equal Employment Opportunity department and reminded them that there were implications of illegal discrimination in George's behavior. There were two issues: (a) assignments and opportunities were taken away from her right after she announced her pregnancy and (b) George's negative assumptions about her ongoing professional performance while pregnant and her return to work after the birth of her child.
6. Jean should have asked for clarification from the organization about what her job status would be when she returned to work after the birth of her child, knowing that she is lawfully entitled to return to her old job or a fully equivalent position. She was correct in assuming that George's response when she announced her pregnancy was a good indicator of what she could expect when she returned.
7. Many companies are conscious of unfavorable publicity, as well as the high cost of turnover and the effect of bad morale on other employees, especially women who may become pregnant in the future. This is in addition to the concern about high-cost lawsuits stemming from complaints of discrimination. This knowledge could have given Jean some confidence in being assertive with her boss and the human resources or other department dealing with employee grievances.
8. If Jean did not receive a satisfactory response from her boss or the organization, she should consider consulting an attorney about her

options and the steps to pursue if she decides to take legal action now or in the future.

What Might Jean Have Said to Her Boss, George?

Jean might have said the following: "George, I am very concerned about my job status since I told you I am pregnant. Since that time, you have removed me from the project on quality assurance which is my area of expertise. I am also curious about your decision not to send me to the Mid-Atlantic training conference, which I had planned on for several months.

"I had always assumed that my pregnancy would not be a factor in my work assignments and status. But when you asked me why I should bother about the conference, you said, 'Why kill yourself?' and made other comments indicating an uncertainty about my work. I'm beginning to think that you are doubting my commitment to this job.

"I may have misinterpreted your intent, but I want to reassure you that being pregnant should in no way affect my productivity, and I do intend to come back to work with as full a commitment to excellence as I have had in the past. Therefore, I'd like you to reconsider the assignment you gave to someone else and my chance to go to the conference. I hope that the two of us can work this out but, if not, I will seek other remedies that are available to me.

"It's important to me that you understand that I am determined to maintain my career along with my new family role."

What Might Jean Say to the Human Resources Representative if George Does Not Respond Satisfactorily?

Jean might say the following: "I have written you a full accounting of what has transpired between George Presto, my supervisor, and me after I announced my pregnancy. In addition, in my memo to you I reviewed my work record for the company. As you know, I have been with the company for nearly five years with an excellent record of work performance, business development, professional competence, commitment, and integrity. I have reported my concerns to you for your information and appropriate action. I will gladly meet with you, George, and other appropriate staff to mediate this situation in-house. I welcome your suggestions on how to resolve my work situation with George to our mutual benefit."

CO-WORKER HOSTILITY AND STEREOTYPING

Sondra Wilkins, a black woman, is a newly hired fiscal officer for a large governmental agency. Betty Haskins, a white woman, is also a fiscal officer in the same unit. She is unfriendly to Sondra and has been since the first day they met. Betty ignores Sondra when she comes into the office and makes snide remarks about her to the other workers, some of which Sondra overhears. When Sondra asks Betty for information or any other kind of help, Betty doesn't cooperate and simply says, "I'm too busy." At times, Sondra's work is seriously delayed because of Betty's lack of providing information and cooperation on mutual tasks.

One day, Sondra hears Betty say to another worker, "So, what's Sondra's background? How did she ever get this job? Two of my friends applied, but I guess they were the wrong color!"

At a staff lunch meeting, the conversation turns to the news events of the week. A police brutality case involving a black alleged victim is discussed. Betty turns to Sondra and says, "So what do the blacks think about this issue? I guess you people are ready to string up the cops." Sondra looks away and doesn't answer.

Sondra increasingly feels that the workplace environment is hostile. At her monthly supervisory meeting with Joan Bianco, her boss, Sondra says, "Joan, everything would be fine here, but I really can't take Betty's racist remarks and behavior. It's really affecting my work here." Joan replies, "Oh, forget it, Sondra. That's just how Betty is. Just ignore her and don't take it seriously. Focus on your work. Try to work around Betty."

Sondra is worried that she may be seen as a troublemaker if she pursues this matter, so she simply says, "OK, I'll try harder to let it roll off my back. I'll just concentrate on my work and not let Betty bother me."

Betty's remarks, however, become more negative toward Sondra and make the work environment extremely tense for her. She feels that the situation is really unfair. It seems as if Betty can say whatever she wants without any sanctions. Yet Sondra feels that she will be punished if she complains or if her work suffers. Sondra feels she'll just have to live with the situation. "That's life!" she rationalizes. Unfortunately, though, her work does suffer, and she dreads getting her evaluation report. She's at a loss about what to do. She thinks, "What can I do to maintain my self-respect and my work effectiveness *and* keep my job?" Some of her friends say that her situation is the reality for blacks in the world of work. Is this really true? Is there nothing she can do?

What Should Sondra Have Done?

Sondra should have done the following:

1. Sondra should have realized that she has a right to be treated with respect and cooperation—by her co-workers and by her supervisor.
2. When she was hired, she should have asked her boss to introduce her to the staff, describing her background and credentials. She might have said to her boss, "I don't want people to think I am here because of affirmative action. My credentials and background can speak for themselves."
3. Sondra should concentrate on trying to establish a relationship with several of the other people in the unit. She should pick the person who has shown any degree of friendliness and build on that. She might ask that person and another to join her for lunch or "invite" herself to join the others at lunch.
4. Sondra should approach Betty privately and tell her that her remarks make her uncomfortable. She could ask Betty how she would feel if someone made the same kind of remarks about her in the office.
5. Sondra should have felt comfortable in telling her boss that she wants her support in working things out with Betty. She should have felt entitled to work in an atmosphere that is not hostile. She should have explained to Joan that the hostile atmosphere affected her work: She was not given the support she needed from co-workers—or from Joan, her supervisor.
6. If Joan, the supervisor, had refused to say anything to Betty, Sondra should have gone to the human resources department and

asked for assistance. She could have said that she feels she is working in a hostile atmosphere and that this situation is having a direct, negative impact on her work. Although she should have not threatened a lawsuit in her initial meeting, she should have made it clear that she was convinced that her career path was being impeded by her work situation. If she received negative evaluations or was not given the opportunity to advance, she could have complained to human resources again.

7. If her situation was not remedied, she could have contacted a lawyer to see if legal action was advised and sought further help from contacts within the organization, if any.

What Might Sondra Have Said to Betty?

Sondra might have said the following: "Betty, I don't understand why you have been acting as you have to me—not cooperating when I ask for information or help, and excluding me from informal talks. I am feeling pretty uncomfortable here because of your behavior. Put yourself in my shoes. How would you feel?

"Betty, I want to work successfully in this office, but you are really making it hard for me. I know that I have the background and credentials to do this job as well as anyone else here. I'd like to settle this between us rather than create a fuss upstairs. How about it?"

What Might Sondra Have Said to Her Supervisor, Joan?

Assuming that Sondra has spoken to Betty to no avail, she could say the following: "Joan, I need your help in dealing with Betty. As you know, she is rude to me, talks behind my back, refuses to give me information and help that I need, and creates a negative atmosphere in our unit. As you may know, I have really tried to be friendly with her and ignore her initial reaction to me. That didn't work. Then I asked her once if I had done something wrong, since I couldn't understand why she was so unhelpful and unfriendly. She blew me off and said, 'Sondra, *you've* got a problem.'

"Joan, I am determined to be successful here. I know the work cold, and I've always gotten along with co-workers. But I need your support in order for me to work productively. I can't do that in a hostile work environment, where I can't even get basic information sometimes. I'd appreciate your speaking to Betty about her effect on the workplace environment. Incidentally, I think that her behavior has a 'downer' effect on everyone else, too."

UNDERUTILIZED TALENT: IS IT DISCRIMINATION?

Antonio Clark is a bright, articulate black Latino. (He was born in Panama; his parents were originally from Jamaica.) Antonio is trying to achieve his dream as a vice president in a line capacity at a large financial services company. Over the past seven years, he has volunteered for every "stretch" assignment, conquering each one with passion and excellence. His performance appraisals have been consistently positive.

Three years ago, Antonio was tapped to be involved in the company's assessment center. Again, his participation was stellar, and his reviews during that assessment reflected his performance. In particular, he demonstrated an uncanny skill in problem solving, financial analysis, and decision making. He also exhibited skills in building effective teams by using an array of personal power bases. Management conceded that he was a "keeper" and an "obvious fast-tracker."

As a result of his success at the assessment center, and because of his record of excellence, Antonio was placed in the company's executive development program. This program was designed to give candidates exposure to multiple job categories—both line and staff.

Antonio was delighted at his selection and vowed to once again demonstrate his talents to those who mattered. As time went on, he observed that other people of color were all placed in staff positions, not line management. Moreover, as he began to reflect on his job rotation, he noticed a pattern in the positions—human resources generalist, compensation and benefits, labor relations, and college recruiting. Furthermore, he noticed that several of the people who had been in his assessment center, whom he clearly outperformed, were getting critical line rotations, without the exposure to the staff jobs that he was offered.

Antonio began to look further and discovered, much to his chagrin, that most minority employees, even at the management level, were in staff positions. In fact, 90 percent of all minority employees were in staff positions. Coincidence? Discrimination? He hates that possibility. He decided to bring this matter directly to management.

Unfortunately, several of his minority contemporaries discouraged him from doing so. They told him that he would never be able to prove planned discrimination, that he would sabotage his own career advancement, and he would make life miserable for the rest of the minority managers who are "happy" with their positions. In other words, "Don't rock the boat!" or "Don't bite the hand that feeds you." Antonio was torn. Part of him refused to believe this plight; part of him wanted to listen to the other minority managers warning him; part of him wanted to take some action; and part of him wanted this to be just a bad dream that he would wake from at any moment.

After days of deliberation and soul searching, Antonio decided *not* to say anything to management. After all, he mused, "I am progressing quite rapidly, and, besides, staff positions are integral to the smooth and efficient operation of the company." He put on his Brooks Brothers suit, picked up his Coach attaché case, got into his Mercedes, and drove off from his suburban colonial home. "At least, I am still well paid," he thought as he pulled into the parking lot of his Fortune 100 corporate office.

Over the next several weeks, however, Antonio could not help noticing that his white counterparts are getting greater exposure not only to operations, finance, and marketing but also to the ever-increasing international marketplace. Just as he was lamenting his lack of opportunity in the key areas of the corporation, his boss walked into his office, closed the door and told Antonio that he was going to be transferred to a "line" position—director of community affairs. In other words, Antonio was to work in the minority community and increase the company's image there. His Latino and African-American background was seen as a natural for this slot. Another conundrum for Antonio! Should he have been excited by the opportunity, which offered a salary increase and a "director" title? Or should he have been disappointed at this obvious and typical "tracking" for a minority employee? He smiled at his boss and said, "Thank you for the opportunity."

Antonio thought, "Am I the victim of organizational discrimination? Can you be discriminated against if you are getting positive performance appraisals, significant pay increments, and increased responsibility? Do I really have anything to complain about? Shouldn't I be grateful for my good job, handsome salary, and participation in the executive development program?"

What Should Antonio Have Done?

Antonio should have done the following:

1. Antonio should have realized, first of all, that getting positive performance appraisals is not necessarily an indication of a lack of systemic discrimination. The bottom line is whether his mobility in the organization matched his performance record.
2. Antonio should have gathered as much empirical data as possible and approached management with his "observations" about minority positions in the organization.
3. Antonio should have questioned management about his observation that he and others like him seemed to be tracked into staff positions or line positions that are traditionally considered "ghettoized" and often reserved exclusively for minorities and females.
4. If not satisfied, Antonio should have seriously examined his "golden handcuffs" and decided whether to (a) accept his plight in life, (2) try to maximize pressure within the organization to have them offer him a line position that matched the full range of his proven abilities and experience, (3) seek legal redress, or (4) leave.
5. If Antonio was convinced of systemic and personal discrimination, he should have decided if he wanted to pursue legal action after weighing all the pros and cons. If he was able to find a better job elsewhere, taking that job would have been the easier route.

What Should Antonio Have Said?

Antonio could have approached a human resources or Equal Employment Opportunity director and said, "It appears to me that the minority employees are tracked into staff positions. Here is what I've noticed. [Show documentation.] As you can see from my data, this appears to be true. In addition, I scored quite well at the assessment center and have not had the same rotations as other, less-qualified white employees. I am concerned that I've been passed over for the fast-track assignments and would like to understand why this is happening. I have a commitment to the company, but only if there is a future for me in the executive ranks."

If Antonio sensed that the response is evasive, vague, and bureaucratic, he should have indicated his dissatisfaction and might have said, "I am troubled by your response, and I need to carefully think about my options now. As much as I enjoy working here, it appears that my talents may not be appreciated, so I'll have to make some critical decisions. Let's meet in a week. Hopefully, you can work out a more satisfactory career ladder for me."

SUCCESS STORIES

ASSERTIVELY ASKING FOR WHAT YOU DESERVE

Fernando Soto, a fifty-year-old Latino case manager in a nonprofit organization, recounted how he became aware that his salary was below that of other colleagues in his field. Describing his experience, he said, "Although most people are reluctant to talk about their salaries, I had a few friends in similar positions whom I did feel comfortable with. I decided to ask them about their salaries, and that's when I learned that mine was lower than average. I remembered that when I came to the job four years previously, I had asked about the range of salary. I was willing to start at the lower end of the range because the job was interesting and challenging, and I had recently changed fields. I assumed that I would receive raises along the way, at least within the salary range mentioned to me when I was hired.

"When I met this year with my supervisor for my annual performance appraisal, I was glad that my ratings in every category were very good to excellent. In addition to my regular work, I was also responsible for bringing many new clients to the agency and for starting several new programs that everyone praised a lot.

"I had a good relationship with my boss, but he made excuses in the previous two years about why the agency couldn't provide me with larger increases in salary.

"Finally, this year I decided to be more assertive during my performance appraisal. I said to my boss, Ralph Lipton, 'With all the project concerns you are facing now, I realize that my salary may be just an oversight. However, I am really concerned about my salary here. My performance reviews have been very good or excellent for the past few years, and I appreciate your very positive comments about my work, but my salary just doesn't match my work evaluations and my contribution to the organization. I am still in the bottom range of the scale for this position, but my background, experience, and performance clearly merit a large increase. I know you'll have to think about this and discuss it with the finance committee, but I'd like you to get back to me as soon as possible. This is very important to me. I really like working in the agency, but in fairness to myself, I know I have to be paid appropriately in relation to other people in this agency and in our field.'

"My supervisor seemed very surprised at my strongly stated remarks. He implied, frankly, that he simply hadn't given much thought to my salary, although he clearly appreciated my work. Once I raised the issue, Ralph made some vague comments about budget constraints. But when I restated my case, Ralph agreed to bring it up with the finance committee—with his positive recommendation. It took several months for him to get back to me, with constant friendly reminders from me. Finally, I received a raise to almost the top of the salary range, with Ralph indicating that the finance committee would reconsider another increase in the next year's budget."

Clearly, this is a scenario with a happy ending, and most salary requests don't end as positively. But many do! You have to test the waters consistently when you are convinced that you are deserving of greater recognition or that your organization or supervisor is taking advantage of you. Being an older Latino male, Fernando did not find it easy to be assertive with his "Anglo" boss, but his pride in himself and his work and the encouragement he received from friends helped him make the stretch and act in his own behalf. He was successful in using his self. Our suggestion: Be assertive and you may be a "success story" too.

"MY ORGANIZATION CAME THROUGH FOR ME"

Gail Kim is a young Korean-American accountant in a large auto manufacturing corporation who was successful in having her organization protect her against sexual harassment. "From the time I first started working here, one of the men in the department, Glenn Gates, constantly teased me in suggestive ways, with clear sexual overtones. He commented on my clothes, asked me about my social life, and kept telling me that he could show me a 'really good time.' As long as his behavior was just verbal, I went along with it. I am rather shy, so I would try to tell him in a pleasant way that I didn't like his conversation and would simply walk away. But when he began to follow me in the halls and brush up against me repeatedly 'by accident,' I felt that I had to do something more than just tell him to stop, since clearly, that didn't work. I went to my supervisor, described what happened, and told him that I wanted him to speak to Glenn or I wanted to be moved to a different department. My supervisor, unfortunately, was a friend of Glenn's, and he minimized what Glenn had done. He told me to 'grow up' and handle the situation on my own. He definitely implied that there was something wrong with me. After the meeting with my supervisor, Glenn's behavior became even worse. He cornered me behind a file cabinet and began touching my hair and shoulders. I was panicked, but I was able to get away from him—despite his heavy grasp on my arm, which actually left marks.

"During this time, I confided in two of the women in the office about Glenn's behavior, and they said they had noticed it too. In fact, he often tried the same thing with some of the other women in the office. They said he had a 'bad reputation' but no one was willing to complain about him because he was the supervisor's friend. One of the women suggested that Glenn had become even more brazen with me because I seem so shy. We all assumed that he believed the stereotype about Asian women being very compliant and assumed that I would never complain.

"Fortunately, a few months after I started working there, the organization held a sexual harassment seminar, and the director of human resources described the corporation's strong policy against sexual harassment and outlined what someone should do if he or she had a complaint. The human resources director emphasized that the organization definitely wanted to avoid anything that could cause legal problems and they were concerned about the welfare of their employees. I noticed that several of the men thought the workshops were a big joke, and afterward one of them said, 'They can't change human nature; that's just the way guys are.'

"But I took the workshop very seriously and felt that the organization really wanted to avoid trouble.

"Since my supervisor had been of no help, I went to the human resources director and told her about Glenn's behavior as well as the supervisor's response. The human resources director took immediate action—as legally required. She interviewed Glenn and my supervisor and told them of the serious legal and employment consequences of their behavior. She told me to keep her informed if Glenn didn't stop being offensive. My supervisor apparently was very concerned and later spoke to Glenn, telling him to stop his behavior. Despite the warnings, Glenn's behavior continued. I reported this to the human resources director. Eventually Glenn was fired, with the supervisor's recommendation. My organization came through for me."

Sexual harassment is a serious legal issue for organizations now. Many organizations—though clearly not all—will take action to protect workers, male and female alike.

Gail's is a story of someone's successfully using the resources of her organization to correct a wrong. It may not work in your organization, but it is certainly worth trying. But first, you have to know what your rights are!

IS IT WORTH IT TO SUE?

Melanie Sherman is a white female physician who held a position as associate professor in a major medical school for more than ten years. She had published widely, was invited to national and international conferences, and had been asked to participate in a prestigious investigation for a national medical organization. Here is her story.

"After being in my department for over ten years, I realized that my salary was at least 25 percent less than that of some of the men in my department who had been there less time, had far fewer papers published—and in less prestigious journals—and who were not considered leaders in the field, as I was. Moreover, my department chair insisted on putting his name first on all the papers I submitted.

"At first I thought it was just an oversight in the department, so I approached my department chair and simply asked him why there was so much discrepancy in salary between me and others in the department. He said he would look into it, and I believed him. I waited and waited. I see myself as a nonconfrontational person and did not want to seem to be a troublemaker. I knew the chairman was busy, so I waited for almost a year before approaching him again. This time, I was more firm about my request. The chairman became furious, accused me of being ungrateful for holding a position in his department, and said that all of the 'prestige' I had internationally was a result of my position in the department. He wouldn't acknowledge my research or publications at all. Shortly after this, I was locked out of my office and a notice was sent out to the department saying that I had resigned!

"This sounds so blatant, doesn't it? Wouldn't any fair-minded person realize that something was wrong here? But no one at the medical school would talk to me. I was told I would have to have my lawyer talk to their lawyer. And so began my long struggle.

"I hired a lawyer, and twelve years later (!), I won $900,000 in a negotiated settlement with the university. My claims were so overwhelming that the medical school wouldn't risk going to trial but settled the claim out of court. Ironically, my initial request was for about $50,000 and now the medical school had to pay $900,000 plus several million dollars in legal fees.

"I won, right? But what was the cost? Flatly, it cost me my career and my reputation. Medical school, residency, a fellowship in a medical specialty, ten years of research, a national and international reputation in my field, former friends and colleagues who are afraid to be connected to me because of what it might do to their careers. Now I cannot get a job—in a medical school, in industry, or anywhere else connected to my field. I am *persona non grata*. The 'old boys' network,' especially in academia and especially in the medical field, is so tight and closed that no one will touch me with a ten-foot pole.

"I had over $500,000 in legal expenses before the settlement. Only my husband's support and the love of my family kept me going. Would I do it again? Yes. Absolutely yes. Because I couldn't live with myself if I'd accepted the incredible injustice done to me. But you have to tell people who want to sue that the cost—financial, emotional, and career-wise—is enormous for most people."

Despite the financial award that Dr. Sherman received, you may not consider this a success story because the cost to her in other ways was so high. But this was one person's choice. For some people, no cost is too high to prevail over what they consider a grave injustice.

• —— •

"IT WAS A BAD FIT SO I RESIGNED"

Stephanie Brotman was one of only two senior women in a large insurance company. She claims, "My company, based in a midwestern city, bought out a New York City company where I had held a similar position. In New York, I was considered a star. Here in the Midwest, I am apparently considered competent, but also 'tough, arrogant, and hard to relate to,' according to several co-workers who have been honest enough to tell me the reactions of others.

"It was six months after I was relocated that my boss called me into his office to tell me some of the problems he had with my interpersonal style. It seems that many of my peers complained about my 'arrogance,' and one of my subordinates found me harsh and critical. Gary Simpson, my boss, stated that if my behavior didn't change, my performance evaluations would be negative. He said to me, 'Stephanie, *wake up!* That is *not* the way it works. You're turning people off. You're just too aggressive, and people don't want to work for or with you.'

"I was dumbstruck and furious. My style of assertiveness and candor, together with my expertise, was looked on favorably in New York. I thought I knew the problem. My expertise was much higher than Gary's. So many times I had caught him making mistakes that I proceeded to correct.

"Once at a staff meeting , I inappropriately—I admit—pointed out an error he had made on a policy review statement. I realized immediately I shouldn't have done that. Now I deal with him only one-to-one when I spot serious mistakes in the work. He's always so defensive when I bring these matters up, but I have always been right, and he knows it.

"As for my criticisms of my staff and peers, I'd have to say that I am a bit of a perfectionist. But I always have the interests of the organization and its performance at heart.

"Last month, I was called into the human resources department and told that there was a threat to suspend me for an incident that had occurred recently. A number of my peers—all men, of course—had submitted a report to my boss stating that they could not tolerate working with me. There was documentation of several remarks I had made that were considered demeaning to them and to others in the organization. When I read that report, I was really shocked and, frankly, very upset.

"I said to the human resource person, 'I absolutely deny the facts there. It was Bill and Joe, my team members, who made the so-called demeaning remarks and I just casually agreed with them, without adding any comments other than, *Yeah, that's right.* And as to my interpersonal style, I'm no more aggressive than my male counterparts—Joe, for instance. Not only is he highly aggressive to everyone, but he constantly makes insensitive remarks about women. But his remarks are always ignored.' Sara, the human resources person, said, 'Oh, that's the way he is. He's one of those macho types. It doesn't mean a thing.'

"I knew then that I had to do something. I thought, 'There is a lawsuit possibility here.' Why? I had clearly been held to a standard different from the men's. Their style and competence are not different from mine. In fact, my performance and knowledge are at least equal to, or better than, theirs. It sure looks like sex discrimination to me.

"And then I thought better of that tack. I was as uncomfortable here in this job as others were with me. They wanted me to change who I was. To stay, I would have to modify my behavior drastically—be quiet and accommodating and unassertive. Give my boss credit for my performance and accomplishments. And certainly not correct him for his mistakes. Or any of the other men, for that matter.

"It's all a bad fit, I realized. This corporation is not ready for women, particularly highly competent women. I'm getting out.

"And get out I did. But—and this is what I would advise others—not before I got a better job. I called my many contacts in the work world, and I found a new opportunity in this same city. It's a better job than what I had before, in so many ways. Better title, better salary, and, more important, it's a place where my assets are appreciated. It's a financial organization that regards women as highly as men. And my interpersonal style is not 'off-putting' here. My authoritative, no-nonsense approach is appreciated. I have no doubt that I can move up here. There are three women already at the highest levels. No glass ceiling here."

Stephanie was successful in the sense that she realized she had no future where she was, and she took the initiative to locate another job in an organization that would use and appreciate her talents.

Techniques for Knowing Your Rights

Now that we've looked at some typical workplace scenarios and success stories, let's examine our acronym SOAR more closely. First, let's recall that the acronym SOAR describes the crucial steps to pursuing your rights in the workplace:

- Self
- Organizational remedies
- Actionable (legal action)
- Resign

THE S IN SOAR IS FOR SELF

Let's look at how you can use your self as the first step of knowing your rights and getting what's due you by your own direct actions.

As a person who is the outsider, you have to have a sense of your own self-worth as a human being, a feeling that you are a person of value who deserves fair treatment in the workplace. You cannot buy into the negative stereotypes that members of the dominant culture may have about you. Too often these stereotypes become internalized, and these internalized stereotypes can do as much damage to you as the ones others have about you. But it's also important to be aware of how your cultural characteristics can be misinterpreted, misunderstood, or not appreciated.

Being realistic about what you bring to the job and how you are perceived is an important assessment skill. And your perceptions and others' are not necessarily related. Do others assess you as you assess yourself? First, assess yourself. Are your skills and accomplishments up to par with or even better than those of your peers? If you think you're not getting what's due you because of your color, gender, ethnic group, age, disability, or sexual orientation, maybe you are right—or maybe not. Yes, racism, sexism, ageism, and other forms of prejudice are alive and well in organizations. But not every block to your advancement and success is due to prejudice. Remember our first strategy, "Check Your Baggage." Don't assume that everyone is hostile. Seek out allies. Make judgments about your treatment on a case-by-case basis and assemble substantial evidence.

Review your self-assessment and see how or if it fits with the organizational demands. Let's say that you believe your interpersonal and work skills meet the norms of the organization. And just as important, you have checked out your perception of unfair treatment with friendly colleagues who agree that you are not getting what's due you to advance your career.

Part of an effective self-assessment is the refusal to underplay your worth. A deaf computer programmer said, "I had to learn not to feel that I was lucky to even be employed. It was great for me that I had a supportive supervisor who recognized my abilities and encouraged me to apply for better positions. But, unfortunately, I know of many people with disabilities who doubt their own worth and are happy just to be working anywhere."

A Latino who is a university administrator advised, "Don't try to be a good sport and accept a less-than-average salary just because you are happy to have the job and are willing to help the college with its budgetary problems. You won't be rewarded. Don't forget, salary is one of the ways you are measured by others."

A woman professor learned a similar lesson. She was happy to have her job at a prestigious university at a time when jobs were scarce. However, in her third year at the university, she was, ironically, on an affirmative action committee that had the opportunity to review salaries. To her dismay, she noticed that other people, several men as well as one woman, all hired after her and with less experience and fewer publications, were making several thousand dollars more than she was. She immediately recognized the unfairness of the salary discrepancy and went to the department chairman to ask for a raise to match, if not exceed, the others' salaries. The administrator was apologetic and agreed to the raise. In this case, the salary differential may have been just the result of an administrative oversight, but here was a situation where "speaking up for yourself" clearly worked.

Thus, knowledge of what is due to you is essential and not always easy to come by. There are federal laws, such as the Equal Pay Act of 1963 and Title VII of the Civil Rights Act of 1964, that prohibit discrimination based on race, gender, religion, or national origin. However, few organizations strictly adhere to these laws. And few employees know the salary range of their positions.

How do you even find out appropriate salary range? Certainly, few people will tell you what they actually are paid. Disclosure of salaries is often a forbidden topic. However, you should always ask for the salary range of your position when you are hired or interviewed for a position. Other ways of getting information are from your professional organizations or friends in your office or professional level who might confide in you and provide some guidelines on salary equity.

How, then, do you ask for more money if you think you deserve it and have been overlooked? There is a way, and assertive behavior is the key. Assertive communication is a well-known strategy that often works successfully if all the other factors are in place: your skills; your knowledge of the discrepancy in salary, position, or status; a positive relationship with your boss; and your own sense of worth.

The key to assertive behavior is that you will take the initiative or responsibility for speaking up on your own behalf. This is the self part in the acronym SOAR.

Here are the steps:

1. Recognize that you feel your treatment has been unfair.
2. Describe the situation as you see it to the person responsible for your treatment, describing clearly what you are asking for and why you feel it is deserved without blaming your boss or the organization. Include your view of why you are important to the organization.
3. Describe what you want to happen. Remember the example of Fernando, the older Latino worker in a nonprofit organization. He kept reminding his supervisor of his contribution to the organization and his lack of commensurate salary. His assertive behavior resulted in a substantial salary increase.

Fernando's experience was about a request for a pay increase, but the same assertive formula applies if you are seeking a promotion, a better assignment, further training, or any additional employment opportunity for advancement. Moreover, the assertive formula establishes the means for expressing your self-worth and acting on your own behalf.

Be sure that you don't forget to first attempt to resolve the matter with the individual causing the problem. For example, if someone were to inadvertently step on your toe, your response, assuming you were raised "properly," might be to say, "Ouch!" That "ouch" signals to the other person that his or her action caused you pain or discomfort. At this moment, again assuming the other person was raised properly, he or she would say, "Excuse me" or "I'm sorry."

Unfortunately, these kind of "toe-stepping" experiences happen to us every day on the job. But too often we don't say "Ouch." Rather, we tend to say nothing or go to our "buddies" and talk about the culprit like a villain. We need to signal to the other person that his or her actions caused us pain or discomfort. Assertive communication is the best way to do this. If direct, face-to-face, personal communication doesn't alter the situation, then you may need to move to another stage—the organizational level.

THE O IN SOAR IS FOR ORGANIZATIONAL REMEDIES

There will be times when a situation you feel is unfair is not satisfactorily resolved by individual actions you have taken with another person, whether it's a co-worker or a supervisor. However, in most organizations there is someone to deal with "complaints." Let's say up front that organizations differ in their handling of employee situations. Some, particularly small organizations, function in a completely ad hoc, informal way, with no specific rules or procedures. Other organizations have very detailed procedures that cover virtually all aspects of employment concerns. Some have detailed manuals, and, maybe even more important, they have a responsive human resources department committed to resolving conflicts, not only to avoid legal actions but also to maintain a satisfied and productive workforce.

First and foremost, you should know your organization's procedures and the specific people who are available to be of help. Is there an employee manual, outlining procedures for complaints about discrimination, including sexual harassment or other employment grievances? Is there a human resources department? Is there an Equal Employment Opportunity (EEO) or Affirmative Action office? Is there even a personnel department? Do you know the names of people you should contact?

Be aware that the range of organizational resources for dealing with complaints is very large. But it is very important to know the options available to you.

An experienced African-American attorney in a large corporation advises seeking someone in the organization who can help you before you "trigger the formal grievance procedure." He suggests, "Try to use someone with a power base who can help you. It's important to know people in the organization who can act for you. You should know who will talk for you, 'who's who,' someone with clout in the organization, someone who has muscle." He further explained, "Sometimes people come informally to me with a complaint. If I think there's any merit to their case, I'll advise them who can best help them. Then I'll call that person and say, 'So-and-so has a problem. See what you can do.' " He strongly advises people to develop allies, so that those allies can act informally on one's behalf.

Unfortunately, regardless of the quality of the human resources department, available supportive services, and written procedures for dealing with on-the-job problems, many people are reluctant to make use of any available organizational help—both formal and informal. The most common reason given is fear of retaliation and reprisals. Some people fear that the person or persons "complained about" will become angry and will take that anger out on them in some way, directly or indirectly. Other people are simply too shy to complain, particularly immigrants and people from traditional cultures who sometimes feel that the "authority" will not necessarily be helpful. Some are concerned that if they complain, they will be viewed as "whiners" or troublemakers. Still others are cynical about the organizational grievance policy and feel that instead of helping them, making a complaint will be held against them.

When we interviewed senior managers and human resources professionals, as well as EEO and affirmative action officers, they expressed quite a different perspective. To a person, they all expressed a desire to know when any perceived act of discrimination occurred, and they all referred to provisions—legal as well as organizational—prohibiting retaliation for making a complaint, whether formal or informal.

We urge our readers to seek help within their own organizational structure. If you are not sure about what is available to you, make an appointment with the human resources or personnel department or get some informal help from "the power players," as suggested earlier. Your organization should not be seen as the enemy until you have exhausted all reasonable efforts.

In addition, the law is clear: Discrimination is illegal! However, you must make a choice and be prepared to live with its consequences. Read your organization's employee manual or handbook. Become familiar with the steps to take in cases of discrimination. Keep a journal or similar account of the actions that occurred and when they occurred, and record the name of anyone who witnessed the behavior. The more information you can present on your behalf, the better.

The July 1998 U.S. Supreme Court ruling on sexual harassment emphasized the importance—in fact, the necessity—of organizations' having a firm policy in place against sexual harassment in the workplace with procedures for complainants to follow. The Court stated that organizations are protected against legal action if the complainant does not make it known to the proper organizational persons that harassment actions were occurring. Only if the organization takes no action against the alleged perpetrator after a complaint has been made can the organization be held liable. Thus, it is absolutely incumbent on complainants to use the organizational procedures on their own behalf, just in case further legal action is needed.

But remember not to assume that everyone is hostile. Test out your impressions with others case by case—with individuals and your organization. Many, if not most, will probably help you resolve the problem. You can always decide to simply stay where you are and "live with" the perceived injustice. Generally, this last option is not good for your mental or physical health, your productivity, or your long-term career goals. If you have not gained satisfaction on your own or with the organization's help and you've decided that it is intolerable for you to stay where you are, there are two additional options that we'll discuss next—legal action and resignation.

THE A IN SOAR IS FOR ACTIONABLE

"Do I have a case?" If you think you have been a victim of discrimination, this is the first question to ask. A case can be considered "actionable" if there is a basis in the law for taking legal *action* to remedy it. Fortunately for many workers, there is now a whole body of employment and civil rights law, as well as many court cases clarifying the law, that protect their rights in the workplace.

Everyone should know the basic laws that can protect them in the workplace. We will describe these laws in a brief summary, which follows.

Here is a list of the key federal laws that protect you against discrimination:

- Equal Pay Act of 1963: Prohibits discrimination in wages on the basis of gender.
- Civil Rights Act of 1964, Title VII: Prohibits discrimination in employment based on race, sex, color, religion, or national origin. Sexual harassment is considered a form of sexual discrimination under this act.
- Age Discrimination in Employment Act of 1967: Prohibits discrimination for workers age forty and over.
- Pregnancy Discrimination Act of 1967: Makes it illegal to discriminate on the basis of pregnancy.
- Americans with Disabilities Act (ADA) of 1990: Prohibits discrimination in employment against people with physical or mental disabilities if they are able to perform the job with "reasonable accommodations."
- Civil Rights Act of 1991: Restores the intent of the Civil Rights Act of 1964 regarding employment discrimination. The 1964 Act had been weakened by several U.S. Supreme Court decisions. The 1991 Act also adds the right to seek damages and to request a jury trial for workers in several protected groups.
- The Family and Medical Leave Act of 1993: Grants employees in companies with fifty or more workers the right to take up to twelve weeks of unpaid leave for the birth of a child or the illness of a family member. Health care benefits, but not salary, are to continue during the leave, and the employee must be given his or her old job or an equivalent position on returning to work.

In addition to federal laws, some state and municipal laws, as well as company personnel policies, protect workers against discrimination. It should be noted that as of this writing there is no federal law prohibiting discrimination based on sexual orientation. However, several states have such laws, and a number of organizations have policies prohibiting such discrimination.

The hard part for persons who feel they have been discriminated against is determining in each case whether or not "actionable" discrimination has occurred. Co-workers can be offensive. A boss may be unreasonable, crude, or vulgar, but are these actionable—that is, do you have good cause for taking legal action? Remember that politeness and civility are not required by law. Many cases are not clear-cut. Even a case that seems absolutely airtight will probably be contested by the accused party.

Basic to your case may be your documentation. As soon as you think something is wrong, keep a written notebook describing what has happened to you. Include the time and date and note if any other people were around who could testify as to what happened. If you notify your boss or the human resource department, do it in writing as well as in person and keep a copy in your own files.

Subtle Forms of Discrimination

Some of the following subtle forms of discrimination may or may not alone be grounds for litigation, but if you are denied promotions they may support your claim. You should be aware that they may be real barriers to your career success.

- Women or minorities are denied adequate job orientation, support, or feedback on performance from supervisors and managers but see white men getting the necessary orientation of job duties, guidance, and feedback from supervisors.
- A minority female employee, working in an all-male unit, is told that she does not "fit in." Her cultural values have taught her to exhibit qualities of friendliness, honesty, and saying what is on her mind. However, the norm for many male managers is to be impersonal and formal. Therefore, her behavior is seen as unprofessional and held against her in evaluations.
- Women and minorities are "pigeonholed into particular "ghettoized" positions and never given the chance to try new areas or learn new skills. They are often "tracked" in special markets, diversity management, human resources, or community affairs.
- Supervisors who are biased against older workers make choice assignments or provide training opportunities based on the age of the employee.

- White males are denied consideration for a job because the office is predominantly female.

"IF IT IS ACTIONABLE DISCRIMINATION, SHOULD I SUE? IF SO, HOW?"

After you decide that you may have a case, the second question to ask is, "Do I want to proceed with litigation—that is, suing the party I think has discriminated against me?" Clearly, you should consider this option only after you have unsuccessfully (1) tried to deal directly with the person or persons who have taken discriminatory behavior toward you and/or (2) contacted high-level persons, including the human resources department or the in-house diversity or EEO official, on your behalf. If the situation is not resolved to your satisfaction after those two steps, then you must ask yourself whether you want to proceed with litigation and sue your employer. You may have seen newspaper and magazine headlines about multimillion-dollar discrimination settlements or judgments in court decisions. It may sound easy. You may even think that the person winning the lawsuit didn't suffer as much discrimination as you have. Why not give it a shot?

Winning a lawsuit is not easy! For every winning lawsuit you see described in the press, hundreds more were never heard, were not won, or took years of litigation for small rewards. And these negative results don't even begin to describe the emotional and financial burdens endured in the process. If you start a suit while you are still employed, you may be treated like a pariah even though the law protects you against retribution.

As several sympathetic human resources managers and employment lawyers have warned, "Once an attorney represents you, you're treated differently." People will treat you very carefully and guardedly. If you have already been fired, it may be difficult for you to get another job without a recommendation from the employer you are suing. How will you support yourself? And then there are legal fees—unless your lawyer works on a contingency basis, unlikely in most employment cases, or if the case is handled entirely by a government agency. If you take the government route, be prepared for substantial backloads and frustrating delays.

And remember—the employer will try to discredit you in any way it can. Be prepared. You will have to be strong emotionally and financially to pursue the case to the end.

If You Decide to Sue

Let's say your situation is humiliating and cries out for correction. Your boss's or employer's behavior has crossed the line many times over. You feel that you must take a stand for yourself and anyone else who has been in your kind of situation. You are going to take legal action. You've carefully evaluated the costs—in terms of emotional stress, financial expenses, career consequences, and time. You decide that the injustice you've experienced is worth the cost to fight it. And you're convinced you have an actionable case.

If you decide to sue, there are two ways of going about it: using the services of city, state, and federal governmental offices that handle discrimination or hiring a private attorney. Usually you need to do both.

Following are the steps in filing a discrimination suit.

Contact the U.S. Equal Employment Opportunity Commission (EEOC) and Your State and City Agencies

If you have a discrimination complaint against your employer, you must file a complaint with the EEOC before you can take legal action on your own. (There are one or more EEOC offices in each state.) Be prepared to describe your complaint in detail, describing what has been done—or not done—and the parties involved. Also, you must file within six months (180 days) of the time the discrimination you are complaining about allegedly took place. Because of this strict time limit, you have only a limited amount of time to try to work things out within your organization. An employment lawyer reminds people who think they have a case, "Don't forget that the clock is ticking for filing a complaint of discrimination."

If you are employed in a state or city that has antidiscrimination laws, you must file with the appropriate local agency first because the EEOC defers any action for sixty days to give the state or city agency time to act on it. The EEOC takes the case only if the local or state agency does not act on the complaint within the sixty-day period. Be sure to check with the EEOC and your local agencies about the required time limits for filing. This is very important.

Federal, state, or local agencies investigate your claim and then, if they feel that the employer has indeed discriminated, they will attempt to settle the case. The agency has 180 days to negotiate a settlement. If no settlement is reached, the EEOC will bring action on your behalf or issue you a right-to-sue notice. After you receive the right-to-sue notice, you have 90 days in which to file a lawsuit on your own. However, if you file an age discrimination or Equal Pay Act lawsuit, you can do so without the right-to-sue notice from the EEOC.

Hire a Lawyer

If the EEOC decides not to bring suit, you can initiate your own legal action. This means hiring your own lawyer. You may want to do this even before you proceed with the EEOC or a state or local agency, because you have the right to be represented by an attorney during the EEOC or other government proceedings. The attorney, who should be a specialist in labor and employment law, can help you decide whether you have a case that is likely to win. He or she can also tell you about costs and give you advice. Perhaps the attorney will negotiate directly with your employer or urge you to wait and collect more evidence before pursuing your case. Some lawyers may take your case on a contingency basis—that is, you pay them only if you win—if they are convinced that you can get a large judgment in your favor. The cases usually take a long time and require a large investment of time and court costs.

If your case is not settled by a negotiated settlement with your employer, it may take years before it works its way through the court system. Remember, even if you win in the first round, your employer can appeal, and the appeal process can take several years longer to resolve. Employers (as well as you) can appeal on the state and federal level—all the way to the U.S. Supreme Court.

Should you or should you not sue? This is strictly a personal decision and depends ultimately on your financial and emotional resources, as well as the strength of your convictions about the merits of your case. But always get advice from an attorney or an agency about the strength of your case before pursuing this difficult route.

THE R IN SOAR IS FOR RESIGN

Resignation is the last resort after you have used your self to act in your own behalf, worked through the organization, and sought, or decided not to seek, legal remedies on what is actionable—all with no satisfactory results.

There are two alternative meanings to "resign." One is to recognize that it is in your own best interest to leave. Perhaps you've tried every means of redressing the wrongs done to you. Perhaps you have determined that it is a hopeless situation. Psychologically and physically, the job is too demoralizing. The emotional cost places too heavy a burden on you. Maybe you've decided that to fight the situation legally would be career suicide. Perhaps you realize, as Stephanie did, that you would continue to be uncomfortable with your work situation even if some of your concerns were redressed. You realize that there are other opportunities out there where you would "fit" better with another organization's culture. You decide not to "fight City Hall" and to resign from the job.

An important admonition: Do not see the resignation as a defeat. Sometimes leaving is the nobler path. But if resigning is your choice, do it on your own terms. Wait it out and use all your resources to find a new job first.

The second meaning of our letter "R" is to resign yourself to the situation and stay. This is what happened to a fifty-nine-year-old female operations supervisor who was denied the opportunity to take advanced training in computer technology. "Why bother?" said her boss. "If I were your age, I'd like to just rest on my laurels and take it easy."

The older woman could have considered taking legal action on the basis of possible age discrimination. She could have resigned from her job. Instead, she decided to resign herself to her situation at work. This meant biding her time, expending less energy and commitment on the job, and waiting for formal retirement to cash in on the considerable benefits due her.

Instead of facing an uncertain future in the job market, some people might prefer to resign themselves to the perceived security of their existing job, with its known pitfalls and benefits, its familiar surroundings and demands and its pension plan.

This decision is not a happy scenario. Many people who choose this path have the look of defeat on their faces. But some could see this option as a viable solution to accepting a situation that would take too much of an emotional toll to battle. A popular expression is: "Some people resign and leave, others resign and stay." Decide what is best for you, but do not agonize after you have carefully considered your choices. Every decision has its consequences and its rewards. SOAR!

SUMMARY

STRATEGY 6: KNOW YOUR RIGHTS

Self

1. Recognize when you have been treated unfairly or experienced discrimination.
2. Check your perceptions of "unfair treatment" and "discrimination" with others.
3. Confirm to yourself that you are a person of self-worth and are entitled to fair treatment.
4. Assess your skills and accomplishments. Do so on your own and with others to validate your value to the organization.
5. Assertively describe to your supervisor your perception of unfair treatment. Keep a written record.
6. Assertively speak to co-workers or others who have subjected you to racist, sexist, or other discriminatory behavior or remarks.

Organization

7. Know and use your organization's procedures to redress a perceived injustice. Usually the human resources, Equal Employment Opportunity, diversity, or personnel departments handle such complaints. Keep a written record of your contacts.

Actionable

8. If your personal and organizational attempts at redress prove fruitless, get advice from an attorney to see whether your grievance is "actionable" or contact the EEOC and your state civil rights department.
9. Assess your tolerance for stress in following through on a course

of legal action and decide whether you feel the effort to be successful in your claim is worth the emotional and financial cost.

Resign

10. Resign after you find other employment if doing so seems the best course of action for you. Or resign yourself to staying on the job if you feel that the benefits of the job outweigh the negatives of your situation.

STRATEGY 

HAVE A VISION

Develop a Plan to Make It a Reality

"You've got to have a dream. If you don't have a dream, how're you going to have a dream come true?" Those plaintive lyrics from *South Pacific* say it all: If you don't know where you want to go, how can you get there? And so our last chapter focuses on your *vision* for success—where you want to go in your career, that extremely important and crucial step for moving from "the outside"—becoming a success when you are not a member of the dominant group.

Let's be clear about the definition of success. Success is different for everyone. Some people want leadership roles; some want to be creative on their own. Some want a cause; some want money. Some want recognition and fame; some want a balance between work and family. Some want independence on the job; some want to make a contribution to human well-being.

Whatever your particular preference, these are values that form the basis for your *vision*—or, we might call it, your *goal.*

Let's look now at your *vision*, or goal, and how you're going to make it happen. Let's move to specifics and spend the next hour or so at particularizing your *vision* and making it *real.*

Write "My Vision" or "My Goal" on a sheet of paper. Below this heading, write what your vision or goal is. (Example: "My vision is to be a senior executive at a nationwide bank.")

Take a good look at the *vision* you have just set down on paper. It's probably a big one. Most visions are global—large, far-reaching, the largest wish you can imagine at this time. Is it foolish to dream such big dreams, to foster such global goals? No—and yes.

The "no" is that the people who have made it did have a vision, did have a global goal. So, no, it is not foolish to dream.

On the other hand, "yes"—it is foolish if it stops there. To turn a vision into a reality, you have to set up a series of *objectives*. Objectives are the milestones along the way to your vision. Objectives are doable and they have criteria built into them.

Objectives are:

- Realistic
- Specific
- Dependent on your actions
- Time-bound

Let's turn your vision into your first objective (which ideally should be the next advancement in your career), an objective that meets the foregoing criteria.

Write your first objective. (Example: "To be a bank branch manager within four years.")

____

____

Look carefully at your objective to make sure it meets the four criteria.

1. Is your objective specific? In our example, yes, it is. The position of bank manager is not a vague idea but a specific function.
2. Is your objective realistic? Let's take our example. If you already have a position in the bank as a platform manager, then your objective most likely is realistic. If you are just starting out as a teller and have little banking experience, managerial skills, and training, your objective is probably not realistic, as a first objective, at this point in your career.
3. Is your objective linked to your actions and your ability to act? If your objective requires that someone select you as a branch manager without any effort on your part, you're wishing on a star. If your objective involves your actions and your effort to become a branch manager, then your objective meets the criterion.
4. Is your objective time-bound? For an objective to be reached, there must be a time limit. Maybe it's two years or five years, or less. Ideally, your objective should not be overly long to achieve. That's why the next advancement in your career is appropriate as your first objective in a series of objectives to make your vision *real*.

If your first objective has met all four criteria, you're on your way. You know where you want to go, and now you have to get there. And how does that happen? Not by magical thinking, but by a specific action plan to meet your objective.

In virtually every book, article, or workshop on goal setting or meeting objectives, these are the essential steps for a successful action plan:

1. Plan and *write down* action steps within a time frame.
2. Assess any barriers to accomplishing the action steps and plan for

overcoming these barriers using your own strengths, as well as other resources.

3. Keep track of your progress on a chart, calendar, or diary. Review your chart weekly, noting your progress and accomplishments as well as your setbacks. If necessary, revise your action plan to overcome unforeseen problems.
4. Take pride in your accomplishments.

But *From the Outside In* is not like other career development books. Here, we have also provided you with *seven strategies* that form the basis of concrete action steps. This approach has been designed specially to help you as an "outsider" to accomplish your objectives. Because you are the "outsider," it is imperative that you use these strategies as a basis for your action plan.

Let's use our example—your objective is to become a branch manager, and you are currently working as a platform manager. You have the seven strategies to do this, and, for each of the strategies, you should devise an action plan using suggestions described in the previous chapters. Perhaps not all of the strategies may seem relevant to you right now, but think hard to make sure that you can't pick up at least something from each of the seven strategies. Let's look at the model.

STRATEGIES WIT[illegible]TEPS TO MEET YOUR OBJECTIVE

1 Check Your Bag[illegible]ssume That Everyone Is Hostile Because of Bad Expe[illegible]s or Someone Else's

EXAMPLE: Action Ste[illegible] Frame:

		DEADLINE
____	Review my relationships with my b[illegible] and co-workers.	June 1
____	Identify who I am having problems with. Do I assume they are hostile to me? How do I react to that person?	June 7
____	If I assume "Pete" or anyone else is rude to me, I will check out their meaning instead of just snapping back and letting them interfere with my working efficiently.	Ongoing

YOUR PLAN:	***DEADLINE:***
________________________________	__________
________________________________	__________
________________________________	__________
________________________________	__________
________________________________	__________
________________________________	__________
________________________________	__________
________________________________	__________

2 Call Out the Cavalry: You Need All the Help You Can Get!

EXAMPLE: Action Steps and Time Frame

		DEADLINE
_____	I will call a senior staff member and ask for advice on how to get ahead and brainstorm about an idea for a future project.	June 10
_____	I will identify two organizations that will broaden my network and make plans to attend at least one meeting next month.	June 17

YOUR PLAN: ***DEADLINE:***

_______________________________________ ___________

_______________________________________ ___________

_______________________________________ ___________

_______________________________________ ___________

_______________________________________ ___________

_______________________________________ ___________

_______________________________________ ___________

_______________________________________ ___________

_______________________________________ ___________

_______________________________________ ___________

_______________________________________ ___________

_______________________________________ ___________

3 Accentuate the Positive: What You Can Do to Maximize Your Value to Your Organization

EXAMPLE: Action Steps and Time Frame

		DEADLINE
____	Explore course offerings at the university or through the banking organization to improve my computer skills.	July 1
____	Make plans to enroll in the fall; place reminder date on calendar.	August 1
____	Use my group membership as a background for a new outreach marketing plan. Complete initial draft of plan.	September 1

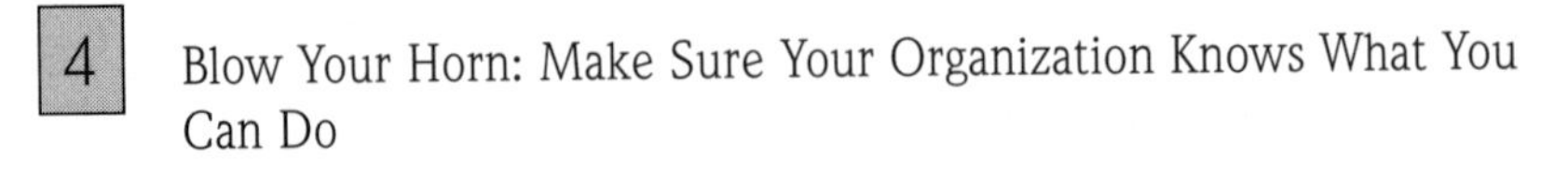

4 Blow Your Horn: Make Sure Your Organization Knows What You Can Do

EXAMPLE: Action Steps and Time Frame

		DEADLINE
_____	For the next unit or departmental meeting, I will prepare a presentation describing my work, with specific recommendations for a new initiative.	September 1
_____	I will join an organization in my community where I can practice giving presentations and speeches.	September 1

YOUR PLAN:	***DEADLINE:***
________________________________	__________
________________________________	__________
________________________________	__________
________________________________	__________
________________________________	__________
________________________________	__________
________________________________	__________
________________________________	__________
________________________________	__________
________________________________	__________
________________________________	__________

Buy In, Don't Sell Out: Adapt Your Cultural Style to the Organization's

EXAMPLE: Action Steps and Time Frame

		DEADLINE
____	I will arrange informal meetings with three or four people who know the organizational culture well so that I can learn more about "how things are done here."	May 31
____	Instead of sitting at lunch every day with members of my own group (racial, ethnic, gender . . .), I will seek out colleagues from other groups, including those from the dominant culture.	June 30
____	I will speak to my boss about displaying ethnic art in my cubicle and how it relates to the organization's diversity objectives.	July 31

YOUR PLAN:	***DEADLINE:***
________________________________	__________
________________________________	__________
________________________________	__________
________________________________	__________
________________________________	__________
________________________________	__________
________________________________	__________
________________________________	__________

6 Know Your Rights: And How to Get Them

EXAMPLE: Action Steps and Time Frame

		DEADLINE
_____	I will examine the personnel handbook carefully, so that I know the procedures to take in my organization if I have a grievance.	July 1
_____	I will request different assignments from my supervisor, since my current assignments do not utilize my background or skills.	August 15

YOUR PLAN: ***DEADLINE:***

________________________________ ____________

________________________________ ____________

________________________________ ____________

________________________________ ____________

________________________________ ____________

________________________________ ____________

________________________________ ____________

________________________________ ____________

________________________________ ____________

________________________________ ____________

________________________________ ____________

7 Have a Vision: Develop a Plan to Make It Reality

EXAMPLE: Action Steps and Time Frame

		DEADLINE
____	Review your progress at the end of each week.	Weekly
____	Complete at least one item from each strategy each month.	Monthly
____	Revise plan as needed, with specific steps to overcome barriers to meeting stated deadlines.	Ongoing

YOUR PLAN: ***DEADLINE:***

______________________________ ____________
______________________________ ____________
______________________________ ____________
______________________________ ____________
______________________________ ____________
______________________________ ____________
______________________________ ____________
______________________________ ____________
______________________________ ____________
______________________________ ____________
______________________________ ____________
______________________________ ____________

Don't forget to constantly review and revise your action plan. It is your blueprint for moving from dreams to reality and success.

Overcoming Barriers to Implementing an Action Plan

For each of the strategies, you will have to decide how you can overcome barriers that prevent you from implementing your action steps. There will always be barriers, but the challenge is to overcome them. For example, in "Know Your Rights," you might select as your action step "Speak to my supervisor about a promotion." You set a deadline for this—June 1—that is just two weeks away. But you dread this prospect because you are not accustomed to asking directly for something on your own behalf. How can you overcome this reluctance to act?

To overcome any barrier, you must keep your vision in front of you and really want that vision to materialize. But are you prepared to tolerate discomfort? Can you overcome cultural or personal tendencies that prevent you from speaking up for yourself? If not, perhaps you will have to add action steps based on Strategy 2, "Call Out the Cavalry." A way to overcome discomfort or lack of assertiveness may be to ask others how *they* have persisted. You may need support from colleagues on *how* to go about asking for a promotion. These colleagues may be members of your own "group" or not. Or you may have to emphasize action steps based on Strategy 3, "Accentuate the Positive," by expanding your skills with additional training. In addition, including action steps based on Strategy 4, "Blow Your Horn," will help you in getting recognition for your achievements. These strategies reinforce one another and will support you in asking for the promotion.

Moving toward your objective using the seven strategies with your choice of action steps for each strategy demands some reality testing. In other words, if you don't have the education or the skills to be a bank manager (in our example), and you have no intention of learning these skills, stop kidding yourself. *You* are the barrier. But if you want success badly enough, you can acquire more skills through education and training. That's doable. But if you think your only barrier is that it is impossible for someone in your group to "make it," you are wrong.

This chapter, Strategy 7, will clarify to you that others of your group have made it. Was it easy? No! But can it be done? Yes. We have given you real, not theoretical, strategies that successful members of your group have used to overcome barriers to their success. You can mirror that, *if* you want to "make it"—*if* that vision is constantly before you.

But, you may say, how can I take *time* to go for a higher degree or take training or read all the new information in my area of specialization? How do I find time to join networks or speak at volunteer organizations? If I do all I have to do to make it, how will I have a life?

People in your group who have made it see their vision as an essential part of their lives. They have sacrificed *some* of their "personal time" or "fun time." Maybe they haven't seen all the movies or sports events they wanted to, or watched TV every evening, or golfed every weekend. Maybe they would have preferred to come in at 9:30 instead of 8:00 in the morning and leave the office at 5:00 instead of staying late a few nights a week. Maybe they would have liked long lunches with friends, instead of lunch with colleagues, clients, or bosses.

But all the people whom we have interviewed and who have made it set priorities. Their vision and their stated objectives to make that vision real was their priority. They knew that, as "others," they had to work twice as hard; they had to prioritize their values and their objectives. They had to take risks, give up other pursuits that detracted from their vision for themselves, and learn from their mistakes and even from their failures. Every successful outsider knew that he or she had to be mobile—to relocate if necessary, despite the personal sacrifices and discomfort that relocation entails.

On the other hand, every outsider who "made it" knew that you cannot bang your head against an organizational concrete wall, or ceiling, forever. You have to know when the organization is not for you. You've fought the good fight, but the battlefield is a marshland that swallows its victims. There are other, more level corporate battlefields, where the odds of victory are good if you use the strategies described in this book and select appropriate (to you and your situation) action steps to meet your objectives.

We've talked a lot about choices in all our strategies for success. The vision, and the desire to achieve that vision, will vary from person to person. But that you can and will "make it" is not in doubt if you want it enough and are willing to take the necessary action steps to make your vision a reality.

We're going to hear the true stories now of real people who are not of the dominant culture and who are either at the top, or near the top, of their organizations or are the first or only member of their group who "made it" in their organization. They had a vision. They blazed the way for you!

TRAILBLAZERS

WHO "MADE IT—WITH A DIFFERENCE"

The Honorable Faith S. Hochberg*

Anyone walking into the outer office of the U.S. Attorney's office in Newark, New Jersey will immediately be struck by the wall of pictures—an entire wall of white men, except for the last picture in the lower right-hand corner. This is the picture of Faith Hochberg, the first woman ever to occupy the position of U.S. Attorney for the State of New Jersey. (The U.S. Attorney's office for a given state handles the prosecutions of all violations of federal law that take place in that state.)

How did she become a "first"? When asked if, as a woman, she expected or experienced hostility on the way up to her present notable position, she said easily, "No, I didn't. In fact, I assume the opposite until hostility throws itself in my face. The realization of hostility comes to me only *after* the fact. For example, when I was in the private practice of law, if an opposing counsel described me as 'aggressive' when I knew that I was assuming normal lawyerly assertiveness, I realized that he was using a negative label to try to disconcert me. Rather than being disconcerted, I knew that my strategy was helping my client's case!

"I don't deal with unimportant slights. Someone recently said to me, 'I can't believe that someone with a career like yours could have such great kids.' I just let it pass by. I don't mind good-natured bantering either. But people rarely cross the line with me."

Explaining her success, she continued, "It's important to have self-confidence. When I was in law school, I was one of only six women in a section of a hundred students. I just assumed I was as capable as anyone else.

*Faith S. Hochberg is now a U.S. District Court Judge.

"My advice to women is to speak up in a group. Break in early. Don't wait too long. This is important because you'll be seen as one of the early players to be reckoned with. If you wait too long to speak up, you'll only get more anxious about what you're going to say and how it will be received. So get used to being out there and don't hold back.

"Women, like everyone else, have to realize that verbal ability is a must. To attract people's attention, your voice tone must be authoritative and strong so that people listen to you. You have to be able to deliver your basic message without being boring. Your tone of voice should convey calm confidence. I was lucky because I always seemed to have a fluid verbal ability. Some people may need voice coaching, and it really pays off. You have to realize your strengths and weaknesses. I know I'm not particularly good at being humorous in speeches, so I play it straight, even when I follow other speakers who tell jokes and funny stories."

In addition to verbal skills, Ms. Hochberg emphasized the crucial importance of social skills. "Judgment is sometimes more important than intelligence. It's important to be someone who can give people bad news and not arouse their enmity. If I feel I have antagonized someone in giving feedback, I'll reach back afterward. But I'll wait awhile and let the pain dissipate first. I also make sure that I acknowledge people. For example, I choose people for the top jobs here. Many applicants have supporters who call me to put in a pitch for their candidates. Some of the supporters may be very important people in the state or even nationally. I'll always call the supporters of the 'failed candidate,' explain my position, and try to maintain good relations even though I didn't select their candidate for the job. Part of having good social skills is being able to 'read' people—to get behind the meaning of what they say. I don't know if this can be taught, but it's a skill that has always helped me."

Ms. Hochberg had some warnings for women. "Don't flirt at the office. That's a high-risk strategy. You want to know that if you get a raise, it's because it's merit-based and not for some other reason. If someone flirts with me, I pretend not to notice. I don't act flattered. This way, nobody can feel 'rejected.' I try not to put others down or make them feel vulnerable. The bottom line is that the future cost far exceeds the benefits when it comes to flirting."

Another warning is for women who have children. "Don't use children as an excuse for not getting work done. You can have an occasional emergency. But you've got to have a backup for child care. Involve your family in helping you out. I'll always accommodate my staff with family problems at off-peak times. But there are highly critical moments in this office, like getting an important witness or preparing for a trial. At times like this, women have to be in the office.

"Keep your priorities strong. My husband and children are crucial to me. I'll kill myself during the week—staying up all hours—so that I can be free on the weekends for my family."

When asked how she knows she can achieve the goals she sets, she answered, "You have to know that you're capable of doing what you set out to do. If the tasks are hard to accomplish, you just have to use 'grit' to get them done. I'll keep trying until I get the job done. If I think I'm not doing well enough, I'll dig my fingernails in deeper. I don't give up. I'm willing to take the risk of failure if the potential benefit is important enough to me."

Her final advice on being successful: "Set your goals higher than you think you can attain because you may be surprised. You just might reach them."

Pete Espinosa

"I had a specific vision," said Pete Espinosa, formerly a sales vice president at IBM, a high-ranking Latino in the company and handpicked to be the executive assistant to the CEO. "I wanted a balance in my life. I wanted to be very successful in my career but have a meaningful family life. Both are equally important to me. And I felt I shouldn't have to sacrifice one for the other.

"I am thankful I am a Latino, a son of a onetime migrant laborer. I was one of six children. We didn't have much money, but my father also knew the pleasures of family life, and shared with us the joys of being Latino: the food, the music, the language.

"My father told me I could be anything. But I was from Iowa. What could I have in common with a Harvard MBA? But the self-esteem I gained from the strength of my heritage helped me to know that I could assimilate and compete with anyone. I was confident in myself, and I could connect well with all people by finding the commonality of our humanity.

"I knew education was important as a building block to success, but I also knew that success is 10 percent what happens to you and 90 percent how you react to it.

"Overcoming all the pressures of my early years taught me how to handle life and its stresses. People know this about me and want to work for me. They also want to work for me because I understand what's important in life. I understand that higher-quality work is performed when you're not burnt out. I have a sense of human values. Although I'm totally committed and involved at work, I know that vacations are also important. Yes, sometimes I come in early and stay late, but I know that if you don't have balance, that if you give up all your family and personal time, you peak and then fold.

"I had to make a tough personal decision. Being with the CEO at IBM all the time was fantastic. But personal issues at home forced me to curtail my endless travel, and then to leave IBM and take on another position as vice president of Northern American Sales for Cambridge Technology Partners, a large technology and management consulting firm."

Pete Espinosa feels strongly about the benefits of diversity. His team of women, African-Americans, Asian-Americans, and others was the highest-performing team in sales when he was a sales vice president at IBM. He explains, "It's because African-Americans and other people of color share with me a bent for challenge. My tent is open to diversity. It's an asset for three reasons: one, diverse people connect to the diverse market; two, they're more creative, their juices are flowing, because they bring different perspectives. And the third reason is they have more fun, so they're motivated with new ideas. They stretch, are more vital and more interesting.

"Because my skills are humanistic as well as technological, people of color seem to want to work for me. They like my joy of life, and my encouragement of new ideas. A lot of white males won't allow themselves to be so open, but I welcome people who are frank and open. My staff can say to me, 'I don't like this,' or 'There's a better way.' They seem to want to test their ideas out on me.

"And some of my white colleagues also admire me for my ability to create a positive work atmosphere. They know that my team works at top speed for me because work is not only more creative but more fun.

"I tell other Latinos: Be happy that you're Latino. Celebrate yourself. Our heritage is a plus. We have our heritage and can also assimilate with whites and participate in all aspects of American life."

Not only did he not deny his background and values, but Pete

Espinosa *accentuated the positives* of his heritage, which proved to be a major factor in his success. He also "called out the cavalry," welcoming and making use of the talents of others.

Yes, Pete Espinosa has made it because his vision for himself, his work, and his life was based on his sense of human values—of what's important. "The participation of racially and ethnically diverse people is the key that unlocks a jewel box full of benefits," he says.

Frank Bolden

Frank Bolden, attorney and corporate vice president, is one of the highest-ranking African-Americans at Johnson & Johnson, the large pharmaceuticals company. He said he's always had a vision of being in a leadership position and of being successful. "I knew I wanted to give my family a comfortable lifestyle and give my children a top-notch education. Family has always been the number one priority for me. I wasn't sure, though, what direction the success would take. In that sense, I did not have a clear vision. I've been lucky. Things have come my way," he said modestly.

His first job after graduation from Columbia University School of Law was at a high-powered Wall Street law firm. But it did not take him long to realize that, with the long hours and intense pressure, he had to make a decision. "If I decided to stay at the firm, I would probably lose my family," he said. "I decided to leave when a former colleague, who resigned from the firm on the eve of becoming partner to take a position in the law department at Johnson & Johnson, told me of an opportunity at J & J.

"Financially, taking a corporate job was a tremendous sacrifice. The average for partners at the firm was $1,500,000 a year. I knew that could be a goal for me. But I felt that, although I have my career, I'm a father, too. My family comes first." Several years after he left, the law firm told him, "We'd like you to come back." Search firms periodically called to offer lucrative jobs in corporate law firms. But by that time he had a clear vision that he wanted a job that wouldn't preclude his spending time with his family.

He described another part of this vision that determined his decision to leave the law firm. "I wanted to make a contribution to my race, to help blacks have a bigger piece of the American pie. My position at

J & J allowed me to do that. When I started in the law department, I worked with human resources people to develop a strong Equal Employment Opportunity and affirmative action agenda. I made a difference for a lot of people at the company, and in business outside the company, too. Since J & J encourages executives to be active in the community, I was involved in many outside activities. I was on the board of directors at Union County (N.J.) Community College and played a role in initiating a program there for recruiting blacks and Hispanics. I'm chairman of the board at the University of Vermont, my alma mater, where efforts to improve the diversity of students, staff, and faculty are being addressed, and I have been on state commissions on gender issues. I've helped find jobs for other attorneys—at J & J and throughout the community."

So this was part of Mr. Bolden's vision—being professionally and financially successful and making a contribution to the African-American community. His job at J & J allowed him to do both.

His advice for becoming successful tapped into the strategies mentioned in this book. "Many blacks assume that whites are out to get them; if they can't get over that, they won't succeed in corporate America. That attitude affects other blacks on the job, and it becomes a cancer. I've always advocated a 'wait and see' attitude. You need to get evidence, be discerning, before you make an issue out of something. Because of my journey from the segregated South to the Brooklyn melting pot, I've always tried to work things out. When you hear something offensive, you have to pick the time and the people to deal with the offense. If you respond all the time, you'll get labeled. You can't be sensitive all the time. Sometimes you do get so tired of doing this that you want to give up. But you have to maintain relationships with people and keep up a dialogue. Often, if whites feel hurt by the implication that they are racist or prejudiced, the dialogue is shut off.

"A key part of being a success is to develop relationships so that you know the big picture of the organization. You have to pay attention to people. Thank people all the time by sending an e-mail saying, 'It was great to meet with you and hear your ideas.'

"You must realize that meetings are your one chance to make an impression. At every meeting you go to, you should make a contribution. People should know it's your idea. If you're passed over, point it out to the group. When I've done this, some people simply didn't even realize they had overlooked my idea. One of my bosses was a quick study. He observed the phenomenon and said, 'Let's follow up on Frank's idea.'

"Don't get discouraged if your idea is passed over. Keep on contributing. You can follow up the meeting with an e-mail to a key person. You might say, 'Here are some additional thoughts from our meeting last week.'

"I tell young people that they have to have a vision if they want to succeed. I ask them, 'What do you want to have when you hang up your spurs? When you stop working, where do you want to be? And then, do you know what to do to get you where you want to go?' You have to make the right choices that will move you forward—for the long haul. The job paying you the most may not be the best one to project you forward in the long run. Dream big. Your options will shrink further down the line. Before you're locked in, make intentional choices. You can be a floater or you can direct your career. If you float, you can get 'dead-ended' without even knowing it. Having a vision helps you select options. Headhunters frequently called me about lucrative jobs. But I knew where I wanted to go and what I wanted to do with my life."

Frank Bolden's vision determined the kind of success he wanted and attained!

David Steward*

"Making it is about making it on my own terms," says David Steward, who was president and CEO of *TV Guide*, America's number-one-selling weekly magazine. He was also honored with the American Advertising Federation's Hall of Achievement award for outstanding career achievement with measurable results. These notable achievements are unusual for someone only forty years old—even for a white male. Even more unusual is the fact that Mr. Steward is gay and does not hide the fact.

"At my first interview for the *TV Guide* position, I told News Corporation executives that I'm gay, in response to a question about why I didn't work to work in a particular company. My response was that I didn't think it was a good growth environment for a gay man. There was no posturing about the issue. This is because I'm comfortable about being gay. But I don't think it's vital to state that I'm gay at the outset of a job interview, unless it will have any relevance to the job itself." When asked whether this was an unusual stance, he replied, "Successful people rewrite the rules. They get where they are by changing, not simply *following,* the rules."

*David Steward is now CEO of a new Internet company.

He accounts for his success in a number of ways. "Vision is very important. I knew very early that I wanted to run things. Being head of *TV Guide* at forty years old was a great accomplishment. I'm extremely success-driven and competitive and want to win at whatever I take on. I call it 'relentless competency.'

"Early in my career, I decided to choose a friendly environment. That's why I chose to work in media. When I graduated from a top graduate school (the University of Chicago) with an MBA, I specifically rejected the world of investment banking because I felt the environment would be too difficult for gays.

"Like football, there are two ways to play to be successful. One is the way the huge linebackers do it. Push, push, push. That's never the way I worked. If I see a block, I find a creative way around it. There are always blocks—you're too young, you're too outspoken, you're gay. You have to learn to deal with that.

"What's helped me is that I know who I am. I know what I can deliver. I know I have a high value in the marketplace. I'm a great business analyst and can crunch numbers, but I'm also a creative problem solver. A strength of mine is that I brought a quantitative background to the media business. I was one of the first strong finance people in a media position. To be successful you have to understand your work. That's what it's all about.

"The more clearly results can be linked to you, the more you'll be OK. If you can bring in the bucks, the organization will be happy. The focus in business now is on results. In the old days, business was often relationship-driven. Now it's results-driven. You can't afford to eliminate someone because they're gay, or black, or whatever, if they are 'bringing home the bacon.'

"There is something about being 'out.' You learn that you live without a lot of fear. You're willing to take risks and chances. Too many gay men and lesbians play it safe. They don't want to deal with straight people. Many gays don't want to work where it's not 100 percent OK to be yourself all the time. They won't take a risk. They stay in the background—lie low.

"I've always wanted to be myself, but to work in the mainstream media business. As a leader, it's important to hire the best people, not the best man, best lesbian, best African-American, etc. Just the best.

"If you have a very clear vision and want to be a major force in the industry, you will tolerate discomfort. People ask me, 'Wouldn't you rather spend more time at home than work so hard?' But my vision drives me. Most very successful people are driven by their goals and dreams and will plow through obstacles to achieve them."

When asked how he deals with the discomfort he might encounter by being known as gay, Mr. Steward responded, "It's like letting the bad guys win if I don't pursue opportunities where there's a possibility of running into prejudice. Anyway, I don't run into hostility that much. Or maybe I just don't see it if it's there."

He reflects that he rarely, if ever, hears negative gay jokes in the workplace. He adds, "Maybe that's because I have zero tolerance for any type of racial, sexist, or bigoted remarks. It's wrong. It's a huge moral issue for me. Everyone knows I don't brook it at any level. It's something I was raised to believe in."

David Steward had no mentors along the way. "I didn't expect anyone to help me. My attitude is, 'I deliver for you. You take care of me.' I would have liked to have had a mentor," he continued, "but there just weren't any when I was coming up. To be 'out' and in the position I'm in is rare.

"It's important for gays to have our heroes, to have people we admire. It was tremendously important for me when David Geffen, the media mogul, came out. Successful 'out' gay and lesbian executives are still very unusual. We're called the 'velvet mafia.' "

David Steward has a vision that drives his career. He sets the standard of excellence and value for himself. He is self-accepting of being gay, and so he is free to take risks, and he sets the model of focusing on quality.

It seems clear that the key to Mr. Steward's success is the excellence and quality he brings to his position. His marketplace "value" and his self-acceptance make being gay a nonexistent issue.

Commissioner Paul Steven Miller

Commissioner Paul Steven Miller, at this writing one of the five members of the federal Equal Employment Opportunity Commission (EEOC), the agency that enforces federal employment discrimination laws, is one of the most accomplished persons with a disability in the country today. He was born with dwarfism, and therefore, his physical difference is always obvious. There were few role models for him and few mentors. He went it alone, but only at first. His goal was to attain excellence and to make a contribution to the public good. When he became a respected attorney and admired for his judgment, his organizational ability, and his speaking and writing skills, he was given numerous awards and high-level career opportunities.

But first he had a vision for himself. He could look nowhere for a person with the same experience as a dwarf and goals as he had. No one at the University of Pennsylvania or the Harvard Law School, which he attended, looked like him. No one had traveled the career path that he sought to travel and could understand his experience and perspective of being a dwarf. His parents wisely knew that credentials were the starting point in demonstrating one's excellence. And admittance to and graduation from an outstanding institution was the first step and, to Paul Miller, an essential beginning.

And yet, graduation from an Ivy League school didn't guarantee him an offer of employment. In fact, discrimination prevented him from getting a job. Ultimately, it was his contacts, friends he had made in school who knew his abilities, who asked around and found him work in an established mainstream law firm.

"When I entered the work world, I first became a part of the corporate legal community," he said. "Corporate experience can be important if you are going to work in the government or nonprofit sector where budgets and resources are limited. Working in the for-profit world teaches you job skills under conditions in which plenty of resources are available to you. Thus, when you work within a system where resources are limited, like the government or nonprofit world, you know what kind of work product to strive for.

"My job opportunities came through personal contacts and relationships. I became involved in the community, and people became aware of my abilities and learned of my career interests. Although I look very different from most in the mainstream, I was able to succeed because people had gotten a chance to get to know me and know what I am capable of.

"In the disabled community no one personifies the whole community because there are so many different kinds of disabilities. The acceptance of people with disabilities is a slow process, an invisible revolution. After all, federal law began protecting the civil rights of people with disabilities only in 1973, and then only in a very limited way with the passage of the Rehabilitation Act. The Americans with Disabilities Act (ADA), which became effective in 1992, was a major advance for the civil rights of people with disabilities. Following the passage of the ADA, I joined the federal government in the new Clinton administration."

Paul Miller accentuated his positives. He became active in the community, both civic and legal. As a member of the *Harvard Civil Rights Liberties Law Review* and a writer whose scholarly work has appeared in many prestigious publications, he reached an audience that could understand and learn from his ideas. These were the academic community and eminent lawyers in the private and public sectors.

Having a vision is a process. Part of that is connection to others and acknowledgment of others. Commissioner Miller said, "I constantly meet and come into contact with many, many people throughout the country and around the world at speeches I give and meetings I attend. Everyone who gives me his or her business card, whom I have spoken to, I try to acknowledge. I write a note to them about our mutual interests and offer assistance at a future date, if my ideas are needed. Later, I try to stay in touch by sending them articles or items that I run across that I think may be of interest to them.

"I expect nothing in return. But many people do write me and thank me for remembering them. I try not to let people fall through the cracks. In every city in which I speak or lecture, I have personal contacts through others I have met."

Commissioner Paul Steven Miller is a trailblazer. His membership in the disabled community is an important part of who he is.

Josie Cruz Natori

Ask almost any successful Asian-American businessperson to name an outstanding Asian-American woman and the name immediately mentioned is Josie Natori's. After the name is mentioned, the same explanation is usually given: "Not only does she now own a multimillion-dollar international clothing and design company, but she was the first Asian-American woman to have a senior position in the securities industry." Not only was she the first Asian-American woman to have a senior position on Wall Street, but the first woman—Asian or white—to be a vice president of investment banking at Merrill Lynch. And she did this when she was in her twenties. "I was the only woman out of 120 investment bankers, and I was practically the only person in investment banking at Merrill Lynch without an MBA," she added. This was back in the 1970s, when the securities industry had few women at all, not to mention Asian-American women.

Did she have a vision for success? She claims, "I did not have a specific vision about being in the financial industry, but I always knew I would do something connected with business. And it was assumed in my family that I would be an achiever. In my family in the Philippines there were no restrictions on women. We are achievers, and the success of children is the success of the family. I saw no limits on myself as a woman." When asked about discrimination, Ms. Natori says she did not experience any. "If it was there, I ignored it. I was too busy concentrating on my work."

This may have accounted for her success on her first job fresh out of college. After working at Bache Securities (later Prudential-Bache) for only six months, she was asked to help open a Bache office in Manila. She was responsible for hiring twenty people, was the sole broker, and virtually ran the office. "I was working incredibly hard because of the difference in time between the markets in the U.S. and in Asia." Asked to account for her success, she simply stated, "My ability and leadership were recognized early." After two years, she returned to the United States and took the job at Merrill Lynch. She rose there quickly, she explained, because, "I had a good track record, was a good team player, and people liked me."

Could she have achieved even more at the securities firm? "Absolutely," she said. "But I left the firm because I like to be challenged and motivated, and I was no longer interested enough in the subject matter to want to stay."

She left to start her own clothing business because doing so would allow her to combine both her strong business ambition and the creative, artistic side in her work. Once in business for herself, she did not rely on others to help her in any direct way. Ms. Natori has a paradoxical view of the concept of "networking." She feels that while she did have supportive bosses at Bache and Merrill Lynch who were mentors, she did not specifically seek support from others. She prides herself on being a "team player" and well liked, but she concentrates primarily on the work itself and her track record.

As she describes her success in her own twenty-year-old business, it is clear that many of the attributes contributing to her success in business also were responsible for her success as an employee in the corporate world. She is extremely focused, energetic, and determined to be a successful leader in her field. She also notes, "I think it is a distinct advantage to be an Asian woman. Our upbringing is to excel. We are trained for competitiveness in achievement. But we are not seen as threatening. People think of Asian women as compliant, even docile, but we have a quiet strength. I call it 'quiet power' because it's not overt. I make my position known—indirectly, but surely.

"We can say things in a 'feminine' way so that it's easier for men to take. You have to exude confidence in yourself but show it in an understated way. Asian women can be very disarming; people don't realize at first how strong we are."

Clearly "accentuating the positive," Ms. Natori builds on her Asian background and maximizes her background as a woman, never playing down either. In background material on her company, Ms. Natori is quoted as saying that the key to NATORI's success is "I design for women who believe in themselves and in expressing their distinct personalities. My audience is made up of women who have a strong sense of self, women who dress expressively and sensually without feeling that a show of femininity compromises intellectual integrity." She also uses her background by incorporating distinctive, stylistic Philippine traits into the NATORI collections—detailed appliqué, intricate embroidery, and detailing.

A final key to her success: "I am a very positive thinker. There are always negative things that happen, but I like to turn them around to my advantage. Every crisis is an opportunity. It's a signal that I have to change. I see myself as a winner, not a loser. If there's a failure, there's a reason for it, a signal that I have to change. I see it for the best. I'm not afraid to make mistakes. One thing leads to the next." Like other successful people, she is clearly not afraid to take risks or make mistakes.

Ms. Natori uses her "quiet power" along with all of the other strategies in this book to meet her vision—a successful business that utilizes her strong creative talents and her business acumen.

Faith Hochberg, Pete Espinosa, Frank Bolden, David Steward, Paul Steven Miller, and Josie Cruz Natori are living proof that, with the will to succeed and the necessary tools, being "different" should not thwart you and *may even assist you* in reaching your goal—your vision!

It's Your Time Now

It's your time now because diversity in the workplace is increasingly acknowledged as an important value. It's your voice that can be heard now. Let's use the acronym TIME for a summary of the power tools to drive your vision to its fulfillment.

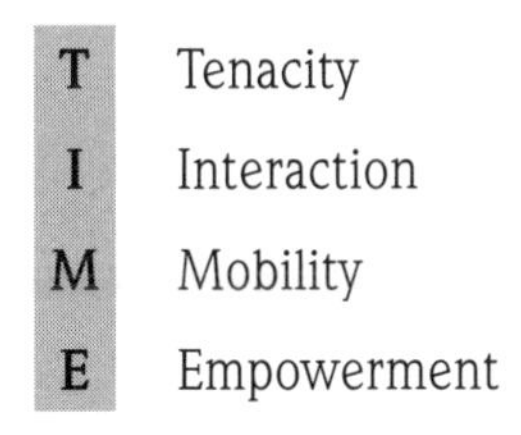

TENACITY

By "tenacity," we mean perseverance, persistence, endurance, staying power, not giving up. Often the difference between success and failure is the difference between persistence and giving up too soon. A successful seventy-four-year-old man says he has maintained his position as a hospital administrator long after other, much younger colleagues, whose responsibilities had been downgraded or who were encouraged to resign. " 'Maybe it's because of my nickname, 'Never say die Leo.' Everyone knows they can count on me to finish the job, no matter what. I will stick with any project until it's finished and meets my high standards. I simply will not give up when many others do. I will not be deterred by frustrations and momentary failures. I also persist in presenting ideas that I believe have validity. I keep making my case. Persistence and tenacity are the secrets to my success now and in the past." Leo had a vision of making a contribution to the effective administration of the hospital and being recognized for that contribution.

An African-American management consultant, formerly an executive in the securities industry, has a similar take on tenacity: "I won't give up on a task no matter how many obstacles I face. Once I've taken it on and am convinced that's it's a good idea, I will stick with it until it's done—and done right. That's the key to my success. As they say, 'Success is 10 percent inspiration, and 90 percent perspiration.' I believe that. And I also have learned that you have to be able to look failure in the eye, pick yourself up, and have the confidence to move on—again and again.

"You have to know why stuff happens and know the difference between self-doubt, blaming yourself, and self-reflection, assessing yourself honestly. Some blacks are too easily 'overwhelmed by the headwinds.' When they confront opposition or failure, they are overwhelmed by it instead of reflecting on the situation and trying to work their way out of it. They take 'defeat' as a reflection on their innate ability. The only true control you have is over your own effort, and some people don't pay enough attention to this. They focus on innate ability and luck, instead of on their own effort."

Remember the role models we have given you. They all "stuck to it." They accomplished their goals by not giving up, by staying in power, by "doing it their way," by "grit." Tenacity is the first ingredient for your vision—knowing that you want to and that you can succeed, and that you will persevere until you do!

INTERACTION

I is for interaction with others. As we have emphasized in almost all of the strategies, involvement or interaction with peers, bosses, and subordinates in everyday work and social situations is a must for success. Numerous outsiders throughout the book have reported that, *despite* their reluctance to participate in social situations and the stress they felt doing so, they all knew the importance of tolerating their own discomfort, putting others at ease, socializing, and acknowledging the contributions of other people. Most used socialization as a means to make contacts and allies and learn the hidden realities of their organizational culture. All who "made it" knew that being liked and seen as part of a team was essential in their pathway to success.

Interaction means not only socializing for your own gain but reaching out to others by helping *them*. Involvement also means active participation in company functions and causes as a volunteer and helping others of your own group when you have "made it."

MOBILITY

M is for mobility, in two senses. One is the ability to relocate if necessary, and the other is your ability to transfer your skills to new situations and business realities as they arise.

Let's first tackle the issue of physical transfer—or relocation. For people of the majority culture in the United States, there are usually relatively few insurmountable problems in this decision. But for people who are "others," major issues can emerge that can create obstacles to their ability to relocate. For example, the issue of family is prevalent for many people of the Latino culture and the Asian-American culture and, to a somewhat lesser degree, for African-Americans. Many members of these cultures are closely tied to their immediate and extended families. The choice to move, sometimes thousand of miles away, is often no choice at all. Many promotion opportunities have passed them by because of their ties to their family.

Adding to this is the complexity of where people are being asked to relocate. Many businesses are locating their manufacturing plants, research and development headquarters, and service centers in remote, rural areas. These areas tend to be almost exclusively populated by whites. On the surface, this may not appear to be problematic. But many employees who are not of the dominant culture must consider a series of concerns:

- Acceptance in the local community—and the difficulty of finding housing. If you will be the first person of color to move into the neighborhood, will you be accepted?
- The family issue. Will your children be accepted or taunted because of their difference? If not taunted, will they be social outcasts? What effect will that have on their maturation process?
- Religion and worship. People from different cultures, even if they are of the same religious denomination, often worship very differently. Will you be able to find a house of worship that feels like home to you? If you are Islamic, will there be a mosque for you and your family?
- Services such as hair styling. African-Americans are particularly sensitive to this issue. Not just anyone can style or cut their hair or offer the products needed to style their hair. And how about

food? Will stores stock the types of vegetables and cuts of meat that are preferred or conform to your religious beliefs?

- Entertainment. There are still some communities where the local movie house will not show any films made by African-Americans or starring African-Americans. Music is another concern. Will there be radio stations that play "your kind" of music? Will there be any stations that broadcast in Spanish? Will the local music store even sell the CDs that you prefer?

These are complex issues for people not of the dominant culture to deal with. But most corporations are unaware of or indifferent to them. If "making it" requires relocating to any area that may not provide an environment supportive of your needs, are you willing to subject yourself and your family to possible alienation for the sake of advancement? What is even more of a concern for people who are the "others" is the fear that even if they make sacrifices to relocate, the promotion still may not come, and they will be left stranded in an area that is not welcoming or even remotely supportive. Add to this the new requirement in some organizations that to "make it" you must have international experience, and the plot thickens!

How can you "make it" if you are not willing to risk the challenges associated with a potentially alien, perhaps even hostile, environment? All we can say is: Proper planning prevents poor decisions. Start immediately discussing the "mobility" question with your family and friends. Don't wait until the possibility of relocation is staring you in the face to begin the dialogue. Know what you are willing to give up in order to succeed. Plan for this so that when the opportunity arises, you will already have dealt with these stressful issues.

We recommend that you carefully consider the pros and cons when you are asked to relocate, get as much information as possible about the new location, and, if it looks at all doable and the potential rewards are attractive, make the stretch and take the risk. To do otherwise may spell career stagnation.

However, we do *not* recommend that you jump at every opportunity put before you. Consider each carefully, based on your own, and your family's, needs and values.

Be mindful also that what concerns you today may not be a concern tomorrow, and what does not concern you today may be a major issue tomorrow. Because mobility is often a primary requirement for "making it," anticipate that challenge. Make your choice knowing that every choice has a consequence and involves your deepest commitment to professional achievement.

Review the words of the trailblazers cited previously, all of whom were mobile. Social class, physical impairment, and gender and sexual orientation were not deterrents to their movement into worlds that did not have African-Americans, Asian-Americans, Latinos, the physically disabled, women, or gays in top leadership roles.

There is a second kind of mobility—the ability to transfer and adapt your skills to changing business and market realities. Review Strategy 3, "Accentuate the Positive," for the steps to maximize the growth, development, and transferability of your skills.

EMPOWERMENT

It is no accident that the last word in our last acronym is "empowerment." When all is said and done, in order to "make it" in the workplace you have to feel empowered to control what happens to you. That is, you must feel that you have the power to change what happens in your career and your life. While you obviously cannot control specific situations you may encounter, and you may not be able to change a completely hostile environment, you can control how you respond to any situation, however negative.

The word "empowerment" has been used widely, but not always wisely. Some writers simply say, "You can do it!" or "You've got to believe in yourself." We agree with this crucial mindset. You must believe that your success is possible. But that is only the first step and the motivator for taking specific actions.

You can't be a success if you feel that just luck or innate ability is the key factor to achieving it. As mentioned earlier, the only thing you really have control over is your own effort—in assessing your situation and enacting strategies on your own behalf. If you face a futile situation after trying a range of strategies, examine other alternatives, such as new mentors, more networking, a hospitable work environment, or upgrading or adapting your skills.

You've no doubt heard people say, "My success was just luck; I was in the right place at the right time." Dig deeper. Inevitably, you'll discover that it was not just an accident that these individuals were in the "right place." Being in the right place probably was the result of networking, connections, relationships, or information about professional activities—not just plain luck. "At the right time" usually means that these people were *ready* to take advantage of whatever opportunities presented themselves. They had the self-confidence and the skills to answer when opportunity knocked. Invariably, success is hooked into having knowledge and skills as well as a positive attitude and a broad circle of social relationships.

One successful advertising woman said, "I make sure I get to every meeting a half hour early, so that I can meet people before the meeting gets crowded." She has arranged to be "at the right place at the right time." Getting places early is a plan, not just a matter of luck.

There are four aspects to empowerment:

1. Accept and believe in yourself.
2. Find and trust others and believe that some of these others can and will help you.
3. Aim your sights higher than you feel are reachable and take risks to reach those heights.
4. See every setback as a learning experience and a challenge to overcome.

If you can accomplish these universal lessons, you will empower yourself to move ahead toward making your vision a reality.

The time is now! First of all, you have role models of your group who have succeeded. And now there is the reality that people who are the outsiders are wanted and sought out—not for any moral reason, but for practical purposes. You are increasing in numbers. It is predicted that by 2009, almost 30 percent of the U.S. population will be people of color. Women already constitute more than 50 percent of the workplace. The talents of the older worker, the worker with disabilities, and immigrants whose first language is not English will be sought after too, as the need for technical skills and a strong work ethic supersedes any past biases.

As the former outsider, you will now be "mainstreamed." You bring resources that are badly needed—being part of a growing population representing an expanding customer base. You possess creativity, imagination, multiple language skills, a new management style with an effective concept of teamwork, and a willingness to push the envelope. You are needed. It's your TIME.

Index